100-WORD STORIES
Folklore and History

Banat, Crisana,
Maramures, Transylvania

Dreamland

PATRICIA FURSTENBERG

This e-book uses English UK. The Romanian and Hungarian diacritic characters were omitted from writing.

Printed By:
Amazon KDP

First Printing Edition, 2022, June

ISBN 9798838116918

More books by the same author:
Transylvania's History A to Z
SILENT HEROES
JOYFUL TROUBLE
CHRISTMAS HAIKU

Connect with the author:
Via Twitter: @PatFurstenberg
Author website: www.alluringcreations.co.za/wp

Table of Contents

Contents

Author's Note

Transylvania is a historical plateau located at the heart of Romania. Dominated by large pastures, Transylvania is sheltered by the Carpathian Mountains which stand guard around it: to the west, Apuseni Mountains; to the east, Harghita Mountains; and to the south the Fagaras Mountains nicknamed the Alps of Transylvania and traversed by the spectacular Transfagarasan Road.

A multicultural region with a noteworthy history and a rich cultural heritage, Transylvania is known as Ardeal to its millennial Romanian inhabitants, Siebenbürgen to the German Saxons who lived on this land for centuries, and Erdély to the Szeklers and the Hungarian people living here today, alongside Turks, Jews, Serbs, and Roma Gypsies. These are the folks who shared this fairy-tale land and together they shaped its history, culture and architecture.

Throughout times, Transylvania was divided in various historical regions that belonged, in turn, to one medieval voivodship (eastern European principality) or another, to one empire or another. Today Romania has ten defined historical provinces: Banat, Crişana, Maramureş, Transylvania (or Ardeal), Bucovina, Moldova, Basarabia, Oltenia, Muntenia, and Dobrogea.

Like a river flows free, like the bird knows no boundaries, and like clouds spread over the entire horizon, so is the history, and the tales of these provinces.

In these troubled times, when one's identity escapes and is easily strewn along paths travelled far and wide, let's take another look back. Let's meet the people who can still remember the tales of their ancestors, entrusted to them with the seed of truth.

These are stories lived, legends of why, myths of who, rooted in the days when the populace of Transylvania laid the first foundations in places still untamed, and places that changed their faces, as they changed many hands throughout centuries.

This isn't a history book, or a storybook, but rather a collection of fleeting impressions, descriptive essays, lived truths, reflections, and snapshots of a life lived in fabulous ways.

These short texts are meant to evoke passages from history and I tried to write them with passion and lyricism, and, I hope, wit. Telling stories is the best way to keep the past, this untouchable treasure, alive.

Locations and Characters

CHARACTERS:

- Dragons, ogres, giants, fairies, witches, giants;
- Neanderthal man, hunter-gatherers;
- Dacians, Romans;
- Moţi, Almăjani, Pădurari, nemes, Mocans, shepherds;
- Vlachs;
- Huns, Pecenegs, Cumans, Peri, Szeklers;
- Hungarians (Magyars);
- The crusaders of 11th century;
- The Teutonic Knights;
- The Cistercian Monks;
- Transylvanian Saxons;
- Ladislau I, King of Hungary;
- Mongol invaders;
- King Sigismund of Luxemburg and Hungary;
- John Hunyadi, Hungarian general and governor of Transylvania;
- Vlad the Impaler, Voivode of Wallachia;
- Jewish refugees and emigrants;
- Ottoman troops and Janissaries;
- Sava Brancovici, the Metropolitan Bishop of the Orthodox Romanians;
- Mattthias Corvinus, King of Hungary born in Cluj, Transylvania;
- Lady Zamfira, daughter of Wallachian ruler Moise-Voda;
- Pintea hajduk;
- Emperor Joseph II, Holy Roman Emperor;

- Avram Iancu, lawyer and military hero of Romanians living in Transylvania;
- Swabians.

LOCATIONS:

Historical regions of Romania (included in this book): Banat, Crisana, Maramures, Transylvania (or Ardeal).

A historical region is a geographical area which at some point in time had a cultural, ethnic, linguistic or political basis. Today some of Romania's historical regions go beyond Romania's borders, belonging in part to neighbouring countries. Romania has no territorial claim over the parts of these historical regions belonging to neighbouring states.

Țări, countries, (for example Barsa Country, Almaj Country) was how various territories within these historical regions organised themselves politically, especially during the medieval era. These countries correspond to the ethnographical areas of the historical regions of Romania.

Map:

You can discover various story locations on Romania's map below:

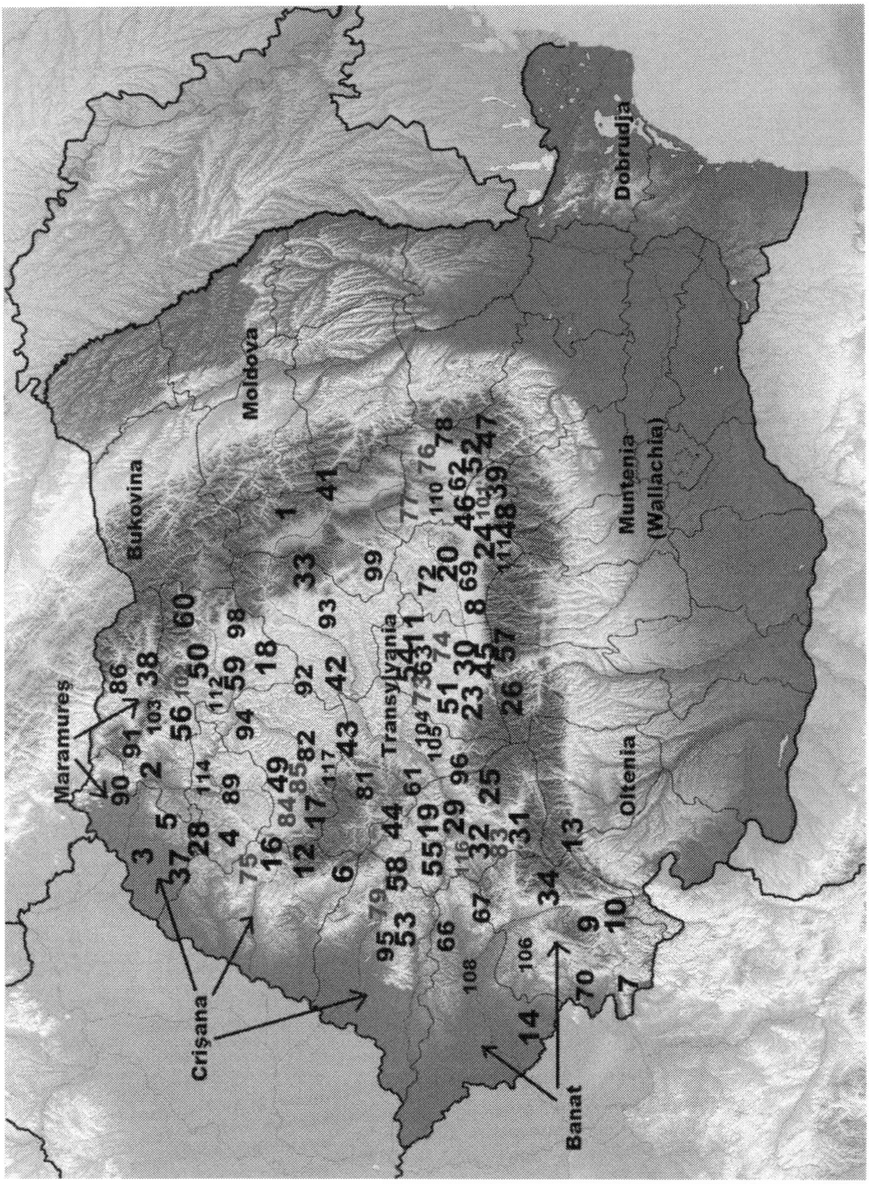
Maramureș
Bukovina
Moldova
Crișana
Transylvania
Banat
Oltenia
Muntenia
(Wallachia)
Dobrudja

1

The Origin of Mihăileni Village, Harghita

When bears grew tails, when people measured their bravery only against monsters and witches, a fierce dragon lived on this land.

His body, long from sunrise to sunset, shook the valley while he snored.

His breath froze it, even during summer's heat.

He'd swallow a whole ox, to say the least. None dare measure their strength against him.

People began to avoid Dragon's Valley.

After the dragon's death, for all things reach an end, wind blew dust and sand. Earth rose forming sunny green hills, rich in vineyards that gave wine renowned far away, just like the dragon once was.

About 50 km from Sibiu, in Harghita County, you can discover *Mihăileni* village known as *Csíkszentmihály* to its Hungarian inhabitants, meaning St. Michael of Csík.

The road passing through comes from the highlands and descends into the valleys, the vista looking like a sleeping dragon's back. It meanders through villages that, today, too often have only a few smokes up their chimneys, and a handful of souls.

If we are to stick with toponymy (the study of place names) and anthroponymy (the study of human's names), then based on my maiden name, Mihăilescu, my family originally hails from Mihăileni (*below*).

2

Call of the Heart in Maramures, at Its Birth

Once upon a time, giants inhabited these hills. One was a widower, with only a daughter, Rozalina, to brighten his days. One spring Rozalina spotted several little men engrossed in fieldwork. Astonished, considering them toys, she picked some, placed them in her apron, and brought them to her father.

Yet he knew what they were, humans, and advised Rozalina to release them urgently.

Alas, one of them had already stolen Rozalina's heart. She prayed to her father to make him bigger, and herself smaller...

How could any father not fulfil his daughter's wish? Thus, Maramures' people are tall and jolly.

Maramureș in Romanian, *Marmaroshchyna* in Ukrainian, *Máramaros* in Hungarian, *Maramuresch* in German, and *Marmatia* in Latin is a geographical, historical, and cultural region in northern Romania.

Archaeological findings show that Maramureș was inhabited since the Palaeolithic period (roughly 20,0000 years ago). In ancient times this area was settled by Dacians, Celts, and Germanic people. During 1st century BC it was part of Dacian Kingdom under King Burebista.

The very birth of Maramureş has its legend. Its people love to share it by the fire of the woodstove, during cold January evenings steeped in snow.

(Above: winter in Maramureş)

3

A Wave Frozen in Stone

The man with faded clothes paused briefly by the print stamped on rock. It had survived wars, earthquakes, battles, storms.

He narrowed his eyes, out of habit. He saw, and appreciated, the great dexterity and the skill required to create such imprint. Millennial old. Art, nevertheless. Bone, tendon, and muscle had been working together within the human hand. So distinctive that hand, any human hand. And a key anatomical features by which individuals were defined.

The child accompanying him lingered by the handprint, compared it with her own, and waved back in reply to the ancestral sign frozen in stone.

The oldest cave paintings of Central Europe might be in Coliboaia Cave, Apuseni National Park, Bihor County. Carbon dating placed them at over 30,000 years old (Paleolithic period). Made using black coal, the paintings show bison, bears, and rhinos, but also a few unidentified animals.

4

Not Blending into the Crowd

Once there lived a man who looked like any other from his tribe, he thought. Yet he was different from any tribesman.

Once there lived a man who was not skilled at hunting, or fishing, or building a fire. Soon he was pushed to the side.

'There's not enough space,' they grunted, 'for one who has nothing to show for himself. Everyone must pitch in.'

The man who could not hunt crouched alone in a corner and, by the shadow of THEIR fire, painted THEIR adventures on a rock.

Once, here lived hunters and fishermen, as this rock art shows.

Detailed horse paintings dating from Palaeolithic, proving the existence of a blooming culture, were discovered in Cuciulat Cave, Sălaj County, Crişana (150 kilometres north-east from Coliboaia Cave).

5

The Bear's Cave, Crisana

That morning he refused the world; even the sunlight caused his tooth to throb.

A memory came; tumbling in warm springs, wrestling his brother then accidentally bumping into their mother. She didn't mind. Never did.

Growling, he crawled into solitude. Leaves rustled, teasing another thought. A hot day tasting of juicy berries; a path to explore, the world belonged to him. Then the sudden scent of danger, the knowing before the realization. The bullet barely grazing his ear.

He flicked a nail over the rugged scar and cried, pain shooting through his jaw.

Time to let go.

The bear knew.

Peştera Urşilor, Bear's Cave, is found near Chişcău village, Bihor County in Crişana province (40 kilometres from Coliboaia Cave). A large number of fossilised bears (*Ursus spelaeus,* extinct 10,000 to 27,000 years ago) were discovered here. It is believed that it was once the bears' graveyard.

Above: Apuseni Mountains

6

Ogling a Hen with Gold Eggs, How Crisana Got its Name

Then, a gleaming palace adorned Mountain Găina. A good fairy lived there with her beloved pet hen that laid, daily, three golden eggs. Whenever a wedding happened in the village, she gifted the couple an egg.

One day three people, driven by poverty, decided to steal the hen. Dressed in women's garments they snatched the bird and her egg basket. Alas, they got lost in the woods and soon the hen began to cluck. The thieves dropped the basket, the golden eggs rolling into Arieş River.

All that's left of the golden hen today are gold specks in the stream.

Hen Mountain, *Muntele Găina,* is part of Apuseni Mountains. The etymology for Crişana goes to the old name for Criş Rivers, Chrisola, deriving from Ancient Greek *golden,* due to golden specks often spotted in its waters. The area was inhabited since the Neolithic period; during ancient times Celtic, Germanic, and Dacian tribes lived here.

7

For Country and for Family, over Danube in Banat

Peering across the river their weather-beaten faces lit up in unison. It was the rugged-green strip that rose against the blue of the sky, above the choppy waters. 'Forests! And rich ones, too. Just like the legend said!'

With tenfold strength they made it for the peaceful shore.

The young mother, basket in hand, stretched her back, yet again, to check on her babe. She smiled at the rosebud mouth, steamed by sleep. Life was good.

What was that? Not dolphins, but locust-like. What else? Pressing her babe's head against her full breast she dashed for the village, screaming:

'Invaders!'

Archaeological findings show that parts of Banat and Crişana were inhabited since Neolithic era. The remains of an entire village were unearthed in Salca district, Oradea.

Above: the Danube Gorge

8

Idyllic Edelweiss, a Legend from Bârsa Country

After creating the world, on the 7th day, God rested.

It was peaceful in heaven, under velvety stars, among His beloved creatures. Yet God couldn't catch a wink. A little star giggled nearby instead of shining from above.

'Well then, I have a job made for you alone,' said God. 'You will beam with joy and announce the world that My son will be born.'

The star shone. The blessed Babe was born. The world rejoiced. While from above, the star chose her heaven on earth: Bucegi Mountains.

Falling unto the earth, she blossomed in thousand little white flowers, edelweiss.

9

Fighting Giants in Almăj Country, Banat

Legends warn of ogres, peculiar in looks and behaviour, taking over the lush banks of a river in Almăj Country.

The people from Strength Valley attacked them, fighting valiantly to reclaim their territory. Alas, were bitterly defeated.

The giants' wrath knew no limits. Soon, the humans had to flee from their valley.

Where to? No land was far enough, no forest too deep.

Only an old man, who'd chosen not to fight, saw the way. Two caves, facing each other. If one was attacked, the people sheltered in the opposite cave would defend them.

In plain sight, guarding one another.

Almăj Country (*Țara Almăjului* in Romanian, *Almási-medence*, Apple Orchard, in Hungarian) is a historical region in Romanian Banat. Banat is a land currently divided between Romania, Serbia, and Hungary.

In Strength Valley, *Valea Tăriei* in Romanian, archaeologists discovered human skeletons over two meters tall.

Local population lived mainly in huts scattered over the valleys because the main occupations was pastoralism without transhumance. The location of Almăj, bordering various empires, made the area somewhat insecure, and often depopulated due to war outbursts.

Nevertheless, its people sang about it, wept over it in soulful poetry, portrayed it in legends, emulated it in the local dance, and even embroidered it in folk costumes.

(A river through Almăj Country)

10

Raging Danube Boilers and Almajana Fairy, Banat

Long ago, when Sun and Moon walked hand in hand like two lovers, over Banat ruled good Cneaz Almaj.
His daughter, Almăjana, was as beautiful as a fairy, clean as spring water, and shy as a deer. News of her beauty reached far and wide.

Soon Almăjana married her beloved and they had a big wedding. But a bitter suitor perforated the boat that carried the couple from the wedding-party, and they drowned.

Grief-stricken and desperate, Cneaz Almaj ordered that Buceaua Mountain be drilled so the waters may flow and drain the lake.

That's how the Danube's keys were born.

Since then, the people of Cneaz (Prince) Almaj are known as Almăjans. Through hard work they transformed the former lake into a flourishing garden with gentle meadows where the Almăjana fairy is said to come.

On moonlit evenings the fairies catch any lad who wonders about. They do so by using their voices, united in hymn, and then steal his heart.

Danube Boilers (above), where Danube has to cross through the Carpathian Mountains. The river's force creates vortices, so the water appears to boil.

11

To Slimnic Fortress, Where a Wizard Had Three Daughters

Once upon a time a sorcerer had three daughters, beautiful and skilled in witchcraft. When the clock struck their time to marry, three princes came to court them, each one promising a marvellous castle built according to their hearts' desire.

The two older girls, proud and spoiled, chose the highest peaks as locations for grand, fast-built castles. The youngest, shy and good-natured, chose the smallest mountain at Michelsberg, Cisnădioara.

"I alone cannot do anything, but only with God's help do I hope that a castle and a church will be built on this mountain."

Her dream, alone, still stands today.

If you travel from Sibiu (near Cisnădioara) to Medias you will spot Slimnic, the old border post of Saxon Sibiu. Built during the 14th century this is a refuge fortresses, which preceded, as a form of protection against invasions offered to the villagers, the apparition of fortified churches.

Slimnic Fortress

12

Fishing with a Rake in Crisana

Over highlands and people once loomed a frightening dragon that had fallen from a rain cloud in the middle of a stormy summer. The greedy beast filled up on local fruit and licked his whiskers after swallowing cattle and sheep, whole!

The emperor promised riches and fame to whoever killed the greedy beast, and quick.

A nomad, locked for stealing salt and longing for blue-sky and bird-song, offered his service. Yet on arriving to the shore of Tisa River the exhausted man fell asleep, clutching his weapon.

Only the beast's roar, smelling fresh meat, reminded the nomad of his task.

Crişana in Romanian, (Hungarian *Körösvidék;* German *Kreischgebiet*), is a geographical and historical region in north-west Romania named after the Criş Rivers guarded by the peaks of Apuseni Mountains.

Partial view of Retezat Mountin

13

How Retezat Mountain Was Named, Epic Hateg

'When wolves befriended lambs, here lived a giant,' the locals whisper showing you glacier lakes as beautiful as clear, blue eyes.

After bloody battles against his neighbours he would punch the mountains creating cauldrons to quench his thirst. Once, after he hit Peleaga Mountain, the Stones' Valley appeared.

But the giant also feasted on people's livestock. So even if he kept them safe, he'd become too much. Thus one day this giant was defeated by a brave lad who simply cut off his head.

To remind themselves that everything has a limit, the locals named this mountain *Retezat*, Hacked Off.

They say that Bucura Lake in Retezat Mountains (*opposite*) was formed where the giant's left hand fell to the ground, his fingers becoming the lakes Slăvei, Lia, Ana, Viorica, and Zănoaga.

14

Mierla, the Common Blackbird of Banat

From mountain slopes covered in oaks,
Such stoic guards of spirits free,
A legend floats like falling leaves
Rustle in autumn: bygone springs.

Alone through life, yet none was sole,
Mother and daughter, two lone souls,
Yet two sums more than one alone;
Mother and daughter, together, whole.

Until one day when food was scarce
Not even acorns left to pick
So Mother left, the world to seek;
The girl, she sang, song incomplete.

One day, clad in her ma's old clothes,
A blob of wax and threads along
For candle-making, pray and search,
Lonely girl who sang, turned bird.

15

Dandelion Hopes

Alone, on the side of the road, a dandelion, a little past, enjoyed the soft touch of a butterfly. The dandelion, until yesterday young and bright, has turned almost white on its head. The butterfly, now young and bright, how will it look tomorrow?

This land is like a dandelion that hasn't reached its prime yet. Still young, carrying its sap like there's not a burden on its shoulders. Ready to release its hopes, ours, into the world.

Are they light enough to fly? Are they unburdened by regrets, lies, deceit?

The secret lies in being as transparent as dandelions

16

Blossoms in Spring

Spring knocked softly on my window, like a branch in the breeze. Discreet, as always when she arrives, she first showed herself on the tip of a shoot, a flower bud.

I spotted her next among branches of lilac in bloom. And among the tulips' closed wings. I saw her slipping on a ray of sunlight. And poking the cover of snow, shaped like a green, thin, and stubborn, blade of grass.

Until the end of time, spring will return and she'll knock on this window again, perched on a lilac's branch.

A bright speck on someone else's clear sky.

Crocus in spring, Munţii Pădurea Craiului, Apuseni

17

Someş and Criş, Two Brothers from Bihor

Joyful were the plains and forest sang when the King married his beloved. Dry turned the grass; birds ceased singing when their King perished in battle.

The Queen, calling her flock, sought refuge in the mountains where she birthed twin boys. Good. Kind.

But draught is like war, soon chasing the shepherd-boys in search of green plains. And their fate. To a witch's land where Sleep-Sickness prevailed.

'Be warned and know,' a fair maiden advised them. 'Only one at a time may remain awake at night. And fight.'

Win a battle, lose a life; a witch will fight to afterlife.

This is an ancient legend from Bihor County, in the northwest of Romania. Someş and Criş rivers spring from the Vlădeasa Mountains and the place where it is believed that the two brothers touched the magic stag's horn is known today as the Stag's Horn.

18

Caring for a Friend, Mures

When Scorilo told me he was going to the forum to play his panpipe, I knew there was something wrong with him by the forced smile on his face. His voice had a brittle tone, different from what it used to sound in the mornings after we survived the cold of night together.

I waited for him to return until the sun began to hide in the mountains, and I started to shiver.

Then, I understood that Scorilo would not return.

I'd go to his house and I would stay there, howling with the other dogs hidden under the bridge.

The space included in the current territory of Mureş County was integrated in the Roman province of Dacia after the Roman Empire conquered this territory.

Various archaeological findings prove that the civilization living here had developed further, and that ancestral occupations had also improved under Roman occupation.

Specialists from Mureş County Museum have discovered an entire Roman village dating from 2-3 century AD at Sângeorgiu de Mureş, according to the museum's director Soos Zoltan, as quoted by Agerpres.

19

Elusive Decebalus and the Strei Treasure, Haţeg

The plan was wickedly simple. Dig a dam, collect Strei River, hide the Dacian's treasure (silver, gold, gems) in the riverbed, topple it with boulders and allow the river flow free again.

They all kicked through the cool spring in the end, to celebrate. In their rolled-up trousers and woolly hats to safeguard them against the forest chill that pulls to illness, was hard to set King Decebalus aside from his trusted men.

Yet Romans found and looted their treasure. Tons. But not all. Bits of shiny yellow and colourful stones were found by fishermen, the treasure of old tales.

One of the most famous legends from Hateg Country speaks of Dacians' fabulous treasure that Decebalus, the Dacians' King, hid in the bed of Strei River while aided by a handful of his most trusted men, ahead of Roman's attack. It is said that the Romans discovered part of it (160 tons of gold and 300 tons of silver) after Biciclis, a Dacian warrior who knew its hiding place, was captured and tortured.

14 centuries later the remains of the Dacian treasure resurfaced.

"A handful of Romanian fishermen were sailing from Mureşu to Streiu and, tying their boats to a trunk, they noticed that the riverbed glistened. Searching, they found even more yellow bits and coins, especially with the image of Lysimachus, the king of Thrace, and with Greek inscriptions. About 400,000 coins and many gold nuggets were found. Taking them home and sharing them with other fishermen, some of them went to Bălgradul Ardealului (Alba Iulia) and asked the silversmiths about their value, and to exchange them for money. As always, the high rulers and their men found out about the treasure and confiscated it. Yet a few fishermen, catching the news, loaded some that passed into Moldova", wrote Gheorghe Şincai, Transylvanian historian, in the Chronicle of the Romanians, 18th century.

Strei River, Hateg

20

King Decebalus, born in Fagaras

The Dacians' chronicles are written on the land of this country, on its meadows, its hills, its waters, on the ridges of its mountains. The names of Dacian kings still live in the surnames of natives, and the names of rivers and mountain peaks.

'*Decebalul Per Scorilo*' is inscribed on a shard of pottery. Decebal, son of Scorilo, today Scoreiu village in Olt County, nestled between two hills bordering Scorei River.

When to Scorilo, the King who held in his hand the passionate Dacians, *Daoi*, wolves-like, a son was born, he was lovingly called *Dece Balus*, meaning leader of wolfs.

Decebalus was the last king of Dacia, ruling between 87 - 106AD. He fought three wars against the Roman Empire during Emperors Domitian and Trajan.

Scholars in toponimy and anthroponymy believe that the second part of Decebalus' name, Balu, proves that Decebalus was born in Fagaras County. Balu as a name is still encountered today in the names of Balea Lake, Balea River, as well as a family surnames, Balu, Balea, and Balint.

21

Girl Warrior

The girl clenched her jaw to steady its tremor. Dropping to a crouch by the shadow of a wall. She held her breath, sieving through familiar sounds.

A lark's call.

The rustle of trees when wind changed direction.

There! Repeated and different. The noise Roman soldiers made as they hiked; their sandals' metal studs giving them away.

Four, maybe five.

Ahead, the sweet slope of her beloved Dacia. Its majestic mountains kissed by snow even in summer.

Silently, she drew her *falx*, boomerang ready in her left hand, focused on foreign sound.

She'll fight the first two; exhaust the rest.

View over the Carpathian Mountains

22

War Science, Know your Opponent

I know these warriors. They are cut from the same cloth wherever Rome sets foot. We think we arrive in shiny armours, on paved roads we believe lead back to Rome, putting forward one metal-studded sandal after another.

Yet they, they have the experience of mounting one assailant's wave after another, ever since Athens was the heart of the world. And they still fight on.

They suckled the battle skills with their mother's milk. Practiced them while plowing their earth. When one dies, ten sons take up arms.

When our roads will turn to dust, they will still live here.

Shepherding in Transylvania,. The Golden Hour.

23

From Priceless Resin to Răşinari Village at Mărginimea Sibiului

Dacians had two observation decks, Raudava and Copidava. From there, watchmen sent signals whenever attackers stirred the dust.

Once, 100 men fought alongside Kind Decebalus; only 15 returned. After them, in marched Roman legionaries. Soon, new roads and rocky walls rose. New names, Râutelus and Copicelius.

Yet these Roman soldiers, natives to the shores of Adriatic Sea and skilled in boat building, knew tree resin; what it was good for. They collected it. Sent it home to their kin. Soon, merchants travelled to buy *răşina* from Dacia. And lots of it, nicknaming the locals who collected it *Răşinari*.

It stuck.

Rășinari in Romanian, *Städterdorf* in German, *Resinár* in Hungarian is a commune in Sibiu County, Transylvania.

24

Dacian Stronghold Underneath Rupea Fortress, Braşov

It was a custom, handed to them by their fathers' fathers, that before a wedding took place a stone had to be laid into the Rupea fortress' wall.

Had their ancestors, the Dacians, started rising its foundation? Only the rocks knew, since they've witnessed the pain of King Decebalus when he retreated here, at Rumidava, to rather end his life than become a Roman slave.

Today, its walls awaken strange feelings when one walks around. The history of this land is cast in its rock for eternity.

If only this silent witness that once dominated the entire region could speak.

Rupea Fortress is located between Brasov and Sighisoara. It was built on the ruins of a former Dacian defence fortress, *Rumidava*, later conquered by Romans. *Cetatea Rupea* in Romanian, *Burg Reps* in German, *Kőhalmi vár* in Hungarian, is named after Latin *Rupes*, stone, cliff.

Most likely because the fortress rises on a rock.

Rupea Fortress

25

Glaring and Grabbing, the Draco Flag

When Emperor Domitian and his Roman army invaded Dacia on a bridge of boats, hungry for its riches of salt and precious metals that proliferated like flakes on rocks, the local tribes fought and pushed them back.

The survivors, under Decebalus, had fearlessly entrusted their souls to their Gods, becoming valiant wolves, *Daoi*. The invaders' loss of banners and their leader's lives blackened their humiliation.

They say that a retreating Roman soldier watched the horizon from the bow of his boat, when clouds suddenly took the shape of a wolf, grabbing him by the neck, dragging him into Danube's depths.

The Dacian battle flag comprised of a wolf's head on a serpent body. As wind blew, it produced a howl, wolfish sound, thus intimidating the adversary. A Roman roads passing though Roman province Dacia started at Lederata on Danube's right bank (today Ram village in Serbia), crossed the river, went north to Castra Arcidava in Caras-Severin, Banat, further to Alpia Traiana Sarmisegetusaan, and then north all the way to Poralissum (near modern-day Zalău, Sălaj County in Crisana).

26

A Dacian Temple in Fagaras Mountains

If each place has its legend, then word of Faith Temple's powers reached as far as the brown bird's flight. While proof, there was aplenty; the cows here gave more milk, and sweeter too. The locals were never sick.

Folk from all lands, some feeling poorly, visited the Temple. Lit a candle; drank from its spring feeling as good as new again.

They say that if you pray just as the sun's rays fall through its tower touching the ground, your plea will come true.

Or nap inside, to wake up refreshed.

One sick babe did.

Woke up in heaven.

The rock temple at *Şinca Veche*, Old Sinca, is an ancient place of worship located at the bend formed by the Făgăraş and Perşani Mountains.

It is believed that these caves were carved in stone 7,000 years ago by the same civilization that founded the White Temple on Snake Island, Ukraine.

The church tower was dug through soft sandstone and it resembles a roofless tower; rays of sunlight shining directly onto the altar.

During the 1700s this stone church was used as a refuge by Transylvanian monks persecuted during the Reformation, when they were forced to convert to Catholicism.

Today the temple at *Sinca Veche* is known as the Fate Temple, the Monastery in Stone, or the Wishing Temple.

Looking up, into the temple's tower.

27

Knowledge, I Am Leaf

My heart is as open as the valleys ahead and as I stroll along the mountain path my foot awakens the echo that's been sleeping for a while. My arms sweep over hills and plains.

I bring you an armful of beauty.

As I stop to pray by the tree of my forefathers, carved in its bark is the sweet language that lulled me to sleep as a child. And so is my fate, carved for an eternity, to know.

I am a leaf in this rich nature that speaks my mother's tongue. Like the trees, the wind. The rain.

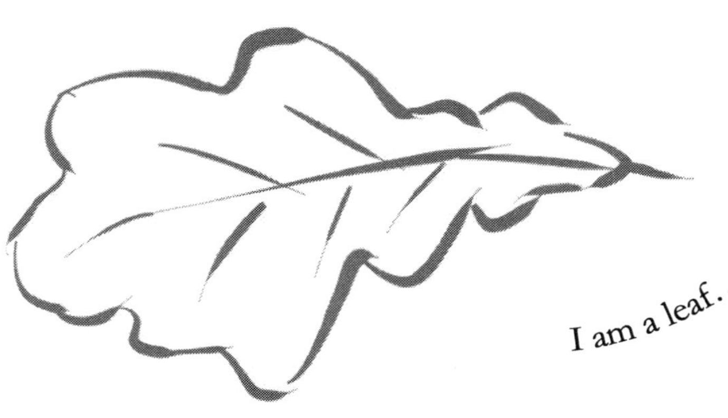

View from Țara Moților

28

Victory's Other Face, in Stone Country

Youngsters rejoiced in dance at Lupşa Fair on Aries River, by Margaia Rock. Only two girls differed; finicky.

Suddenly, two outlanders arrived; boots with spurs, striking dancing skills. They chose the two girls dancing, laughing, spinning together till they reached Margaia Rock. There, a door opened and, quickly, locked straight behind them.

Only a girl's apron remained behind, free in the wind.

The two maidens found themselves prisoners in a lush valley, while the boys turned into dragons. One girl, curious, kept asking questions. Till she learned which plants will brew a potion: curled grass, bastard-balm, basil.

To free her.

Ţara Moţilor in Romanian, *Motzenland* in German, also known as *Ţara de Piatră*, The Stone Land, is an ethno-geographical region in western Romania.

Its inhabitants are known as *moţi*. The etymology of word *Moţ* can be traced to the Latin *motus*, *moti* (plural) meaning tumult, rebellion, agitation of a crowd.

Not surprisingly, this explanation draws from the revolt of the gold mines' slaves during the Roman rule of Dacia. It is assumed that, due to its magnitude and drama, the event etched itself in the local ethnic memory. And as for the rebellious slaves, they would have taken refuge along Upper Arieş River where the terrain allowed them defence and resistance against the Roman cohorts.

Further historical events that took place in Apuseni are another testimony to the meaning of nickname *Moţi,* rebels. In 1568, the Transylvania Diet (a legislative, administrative and judicial body) held at Turda issued for the first time in the history of Europe a document proclaiming the freedom of conscience and religious tolerance (although the Greek Orthodox cult practiced by the Romanians was not yet recognized, only tolerated).Also, the Revolt of Horea, Closca, and Crisan (1784–1785) and the Romanian Transylvanian segment of the 1848 Revolution also originated here.

Thus, a moniker of a Romanian group turned from nickname into fame.

The church of hamlet Valisoara.

29

Escape from Hateg Country

Once a starry night, under moon's golden rays, in her bed-chamber atop a tower Ileana turned her spinning wheel.

And then what she saw? The yarn twisted after midnight was of gold thread, and whatever she twisted after that, was gold too.

Good magic, she hoped, spinning night after night till the gold thread made its way down the turret, to the dungeon where Ileana's beloved was chained. When the golden threads touched its chains, they cracked and he was able to run home, in her loving arms.

She felt his face, remembering the sight she once enjoyed looking at.

Haţeg Land (*Ţara Haţegului* in Romanian, *Wallenthal* in German, *Hátszegvidék* in Hungarian, *terra Harszoc* in Latin) is a historical and ethnographical area in Hunedoara County, Romania, in the south-western corner of Transylvania. It is nicknamed Ardeal's Heaven (*Raiul Ardealului*), due to the beauty of the place.

Haţeg Country seen from Rachitova Tower

30

The Giants from Cristian, Sibiu, Barsa Country

Once upon a time, when seas covered most of our earth and, where mountains rise today then grew small islands, the world was ruled by giants.

One day their king's sceptre fell into the sea.

Lo and behold, they drained it at once. Thus, Bursenland appeared, surrounded by mountain peaks. And a few passes came to be, here and there, the way the waters drained between mountain peaks.

The giant who did all the work was rather drenched so he laid his pants on Sânpetru Mountain, to dry.

They say that even today you can see the mark they left.

Sânpetru, Saint Peter, is one of the fourteen settlements founded by German settlers in 1211 in Bârsa Country, *Bursenland*, that have survived to present day. Research showed that the dialect used by the population living here is similar to that of the people living along the Rhine Valley. It is believed that the Teutonic Knights who founded this village named it *Mons Sancti Petri* in memory of the land they left behind. The coat of arms of Sânpetru, two crossed keys placed on a shield, originates to this era.

The Evangelic Church Christian, Sibiu

31

Dacians Then, Today Foresters, Hunedoara

I've come to the Foresters' Land to see the keys.

They told me they'll be gathered in a bunch. That I'll hear their cheerful clinging, like the blessed bells' songs, whenever maidens dance.

That they're proof of honour and purity. Gifted from mother to daughter.

Today, Ma Flower holds the keys.

She first wore them on her belt the day she married, and every day until she reached thirty springs. That's when she changed her shirt embroidered with red silk for a black one.

The keys went in her chest, together with her red-embroidered shirt, her youthful memories, and dreams.

On the plateau of *Poiana Ruscă* Mountains, among sunny slopes, a native population deeply rooted in its Romanian spirit was preserved.

At the beginning of 2nd century AD major Dacian and Roman centres developed in the eastern part of these mountains; while at the foot of the massif, in *Hațeg*, the Roman capital of Dacia province was located, Ulpia Traiana Sarmizegetusa.

Yet part of Dacians would have retreated into the neighbouring mountains and forests seeking refuge from the Roman conquerors. Today, these inhabitants still call themselves foresters, *pădurari.* They represent an island of ethnography where an archaic popular culture prevailed in an original wat, differentiating itself form the cultures of the neighbouring regions, partly because of its geographical position. This is *Ținutul Pădurarilor*, Forester's Land.

32

Envious Dochia, a Spring Legend from Pădureni, Haţeg

When Dragobete fell in love his mother, Old Dochia, not liking the girl sent her to the river to wash a bundle of black wool. Till it whitened like the snow covering the earth.

St. Peter, spotting the girl's frozen fingers, gifted her red flowers to aid whiten the wool.

Old Dochia imagined that spring had arrived sooner and hastened with her sheep to mountain pastures. Heated by her eager hike she removed her nine coats. Snow and sleet surrounded her.

Soon enough, Dochia froze to stone.

Her rocky shape in the Ceahlau Mountain can still be spotted, even today.

Romania has several legends regarding the arriving of spring with its fickle weather. One is the legend of Old Dochia, a mean and vengeful woman. The large rocks of Ceahlau Mountains that can be seen even today are a living testimony of this legend.

Ceahlau Mountains, Dochia Rocks

33

Through the Szeklers' Gate

It is a song of plane and chisel, of polishing wood, revealing its secrets, symbols that hold meaning to a nation alone, the Szeklers.

For endless months the woodworker will carve a gate and one alone. Standing on three poles, with two entries and a roof, it's meant to last for generations. At least three.

The chisel pecks like a fine bird feeding on timber, and flowers come to life; bunches reach the columbarium atop, the soul of the gate protected by a shingled roof.

Bright paint brings it alive, tulips for women, carnations for men.

A prayer to heaven.

After Attila's death in 453 the Hun Empire crumbled. The Huns who reached eastern Transylvania organised themselves in "seats", *szekely*, meaning those who are organised in seats.

The Szeklers Gates, found at the yard's entrance, have three pillars and a girder beam above on which a dove cote is found, with a shingles roof. They have wood carvings, especially flowers, and are always painted.

The Szekler Gates, as important as any family member, represents the crowning jewel of the Szekler house. When building such a gate the trees that are cut are perceived as receiving new life because the Szekler gate is integrated within the human existence, its wood carver pouring his soul into sculpting it, then into engraving God's name through gentle and pious artwork.

34

Water Mills from Rudaria, Mountainous Banat

The young mother prayed with the water-rustle then placed her babe in the flour-collector. She wished for abundant speech for him, like the mill-race.

'Ya'll kill him!' screeched the gossip-town. Jealous of her wealth, her babe. 'Ya' man's in the country 'gain. Is he swapping ya' corn-flour, or you?'

The words crunched like the milling stone's grinding.

'Wheat flour for a Christmas bread 'be nice,' she murmured fancying the tattletale down the torrent rushing over mill-stones.

Oh, she'd go by the Backwards Mill, turn back the time. She'd made sure her man would return, giving him spring water to sip.

The water-mills from Rudăria village, today Eftimie Murgu, grind the finest corn flour on a stone on stone mill.

The expression "to go in the country" meant to travel to Orşova, in the historical province of Oltenia, to market, and exchange corn flour for wheat flour, as in Banat was too cold for wheat to grow.

A *rudar* was a woodworker; some made the wood structure of a mill; others specialised in carving wooden spoons, or spinning needles.

35

Joyful Summer

With hair of lady's bedstraw, eyes as blue as chicory, and a dress made of poppies, summer bursts on her chariot of hot winds climbing the mountains full speed.

Cheeky, she roused the weather bringing hot showers that only stir the scents. Earth, blooms, wet leaves, rocks, moss and tree bark, they swirl in dizzying spells overpowering those climbing these mountain paths.

Summer's spells are equally potent for men or women, young or old, brown, red, or white-haired.

'Tis enough to stroll the paths of Transylvania, crush its scents underfoot. You're hooked. The day's long, the bloom's lazy, life's sweet.

36

Sacrificing the Ignat Pig

I finger-paint lines on my forehead, a heart on my chest. It's time to become an adult. My village wants to see me grow up.

I step into the forest like a wolf; when I lose my way I am a lamb in spring. Searching for a way home, not seeing it. So my arms become branches, my eyes leaves searching for the sun's ray to point the way. I am just another sapling, sighing in the wind.

I open my eyes to a Christmas ritual that marks me as my kin, while I painted myself with the pig's blood.

Ignat is the name given to the day of 20th of December, a celebration that peasants dedicate to the sacrificing of the pig ahead of Christmas festivities. The origin of the Ignat celebration goes back to the Roman pagan festival of Saturnalia, in honour of agricultural god Saturn.

37

Fairy's Pantry or the Magical Realm of Oas Country, Satmar

Legend says that three outlaws, wrongly persecuted by authorities, took refuge in this forest and settled on the shores of Pasteni's Spring. After their ordeal, a land serene.

It was blessed.

They had not arrived alone though, for with them came their kin, and maidens too, nicknamed fairies.

For their beauty.

The place where they built new life, in peaceful solitude, was an enclosure difficult to reach even for barbarian invaders. None knew that it was a forgotten, cherished sanctuary.

Of the free Dacians.

To them it was simply heaven. So they named it Fairies Room.

Known today as Cămărzâna.

The village of *Cămărzâna* appears in the archives of Satu Mare County in 1490 as Camarzan, meaning Fairy Room.

Regarding the origins of the name of *Cămărzâna*, there are two explanations. The first, etymological, and the second based on a local legend.

According to linguists, the name *Cămărzâna* comes from the Dacian term 'Camara Zana', 'Holy Place'. Specialists believe that two millennia ago there was a Zalmoxian temple on this lands, an important religious centre of the free Dacians. In Romanian *cămara* means pantry, and *zâna* means fairy.

The legend says that when *Țara Oașului* (Oaș Country, a historical region located nearby) was threatened by barbaric invasion the men from Oaş hid their wives and daughters (who were as beautiful as fairies) in this natural hide-out to keep them safe.

Cămârzani Monastery, first established 1863

38

Tough Luck at Lower Viseul, Maramures

Old folk speak the truth, for they lived it. Such whispers wheel in Vişeu village.

From the forest came a girl. Her hair as long as late summer grass. Her eyes, as deep as oak-bark. Her dress the rustle of leaves, her voice the murmur of a spring. Alas!

Her fingers, as sticky as cleavers for what she touched, it twisted; what she looked upon, it shrivelled. As she muttered, it happened.

A village of hideous people emerged.

None escaped. Unless!

They'd plow the field with three pairs of twin oxen. And then hide their village between four sister valleys.

Lower Vişeul, *Vişeul de Jos* in Romanian, *Alsóvisó* in Hungarian, *Unterwischau* in German, is a commune in Maramureş County. It was first mentioned in 1353 as part of the Bogdăneşti principality.

According to legend, the hearth of the village is located between four valleys (Drăguiesii, Secăturii, Ghemii, and Porcului) in order to confuse the route of future misfortunes. In Romanian folklore, twin animals are considered auspicious and lucky.

An old house from Maramureş.

39

How Romanians, Hungarians and Saxons Settled in Bârsa Country

Legend says that once upon a time Romanians, Hungarians, and Saxons lived in great harmony, even if a little crowded.

When Bursenland was finally freed from giants, the Romanians, Hungarians, and Saxons decided to race as far as they could; where they would stop, that land would be theirs.

The Saxons, wearing heavy boots, stopped in the middle of the plains. The Hungarians, in their boots, made it to the foot of the mountains. While the Romanians, in light *opinci*, leather footplates, stopped only on the flanks of the mountains.

They waved at each other and went on, living peacefully.

Bârsa Country is known as *Țara Bârsei* in Romanian, *Burzenland* in German, *Barcaság* in Hungarian, and *Terra Borza* in Latin. It is a historical and ethnographic region of Romania located in the southeast of Transylvania. Brașov is its main city.

40

Pause: on the Origin of Hungarians

Once upon a time, a young Scythians queen dreamed that divine will descended upon her like a great vulture. She dreamed how her unborn babe, Âlmos, will one day rule like a great river of fire over a vast land. For the land of her ancestors, Attila's people, was a land meant for their grandchildren too, the nomad Ten Arrows Tribes, the Onogur.

A mother's dream, a queen's desire, or a prophecy born from thirst for power? Or great leadership stirred the imagination and the legend came in remembrance?

Power is like a sun that never sets and bears shadows.

"According to an orally transmitted legend, the brothers Hunor and Magor, sons of the Scythian Kings Gog and Magog, (…) during a hunt, arrived in the region north of the Sea of Azov. Having lost the trail of the animal, they caught sight of the two exquisitely beautiful daughters of Dula, King of the Alans. The brothers married the two maidens, and the offspring of these marriages are said to be the ancestors of the Huns and Magyars, namely "the famous all-powerful King Attila and later Duke Almos, from whom the Hungarian kings and dukes originated". Today linguists concede that this cherished legend contains a grain of historical truth: the close link between the Magyars (Hungarians) and a Bulgarian-Turkic people, as well as the Alans. While the term "Magyar", used by the Hungarians themselves, harks back to Ugrian times, the appellation "Hungarian", "Ungar", "Hungarus", "Hongrois", is traceable to the tribal organization of the Onogurs, to which the Hungarians had belonged for a long period; Onogur means "ten arrows", signifying ten tribes.(…) However, it is certain that the Hungarians had for some time been members of the Turkic Khazar empire between the middle Volga and the lower Danube. Since 830 the Magyars (Hungarians) had lived, together with various nomadic Turkic peoples, the Alans and the Slavs, in the Etelkoz, "the area between two rivers"—an extensive region between the Don, the Danube and the Black Sea."

Paul Lendvai, "Hungarians: A Thousand Years of Victory in Defeat (2003)". Born Pál Lendvai is a Hungarian-born Austrian journalist.

View of the Carpathian Mountains

41

Play: Csaba Returns, Hungarians in land of Szeklers

When Csaba saw his Huns on the verge of extinction he shot an arrow, requesting the enchanted fairy's aid. His mother.

The arrow lodged near a miraculous weed whose sap healed wounds.

Thus Csaba revived his fallen warriors, leading them against the enemy. Faced with an army of the dead, the Gepis ran, terrified.

Young Csaba led his people to the border of Transylvania, commanding them to build there hearth, and promising the nations already settled there, and Szeklers too, that whenever a great danger will threatened them, he and his warriors will rise from the grave and save them.

42

Pursuing a Life on a New Land, the Hungarians Arrive

The winter wind froze their cries for help as Magyar tribes lost one battle after another against the Pechenegs, Europe's mercenaries.

With their own warriors away, fighting other nation's wars, women and elders were left like reeds in the wind, to bend under its blow, to hide among the grass, till the storm will pass. And when it didn't, left to run away, to run AHEAD, towards a promising land, a land whose peaceful hills and sturdy forests will protect them.

Through the Verecke Pass they descended, among russet leaves, and entered the Land Beyond the Forest.

But whose land?

"The significance of the Hungarians in the subsequent destiny of the Germans and Austrians in this region began to show as early as 881—first when they clashed with Frankish troops near Vienna(…). This account in the Salzburg Annals not only names Vienna for the first time, but is also the earliest mention of the Hungarians from a Bavarian source—thus indicating even at this date interest in the region and in the Hungarians. (…). The decisive impetus for the acquisition of land and for a conclusive crossing of the Carpathians came neither from the search for grazing land, nor from increasing population, nor from the mere prospect of plunder, but—in contrast to epic tradition—from a massive defeat by the nomadic Pechenegs, a people of Turkic origin. The disaster began when the Hungarians turned against the Bulgarians to fulfil a military compact with Byzantium. The latter not only made peace with Byzantium but beat the Hungarian army led by the son of Arpad, against which it used the Pechenegs. As most of the Hungarian warriors were fighting in the south or in Moravia, the Pechenegs could easily attack and devastate the virtually undefended Hungarian settlements. The defeated troops and the many ravaged non-combatants escaped across the Carpathians into the, by then, familiar Pannonia. It was therefore "a flight forwards". Most historians agree that the Hungarian tribes were in severe straits when they set out in the autumn of 895 on their march into the Danube basin. They advanced from the northeast across the Verecke pass, from the east and southeast across the Transylvanian Carpathians, and along the Danube. The pre-history and the sequence of events of this westward progress were portrayed differently in historiography, above all in the records of the chroniclers and in the literature of each of the affected peoples and their later national states. Even if the land, as already mentioned, was far from being uninhabited or deserted at that time, there was clearly no comprehensive political organization, but rather a political vacuum, and the local residents seem to have been more or less defenceless and at the mercy of the invading Hungarians."

Paul Lendvai, "Hungarians: A Thousand Years of Victory in Defeat (2003)". Born Pál Lendvai is a Hungarian-born Austrian journalist.

43

Crossing the Sea-Like Forest

The forest is a sea that I did not know. Before, my world reached south, to the flat strip of river; that was its abyss.

One day I ventured further north. And from blue, my sea turned forest green.

The new world, the land over the forest that neither ends nor dries up, no matter how much war you pour into it, sucked me in. Like a wave that lifts, then drops and pulls everything into its depths.

Only that here the waves rustle in the wind. And I am, once again, a fish on the bottom of the sea.

Venturing from the north, the Hungarians (or Magyars as they called themselves) would have crossed the forested slopes of Maramures.

Geoagiu, Rotonda Church

44

The Rotonda Church of Geoagiu, a Hungarian Legend

When the Crusaders returned from Jerusalem, having rebuild the Church of Christ, they paused shortly by a sweet spring.

Around them, cool forest. Underneath their footing, soft moss. And rising from the ground, river rocks mixed with Roman bricks climbing together to form a rotunda.

They stood in an ancient church!

Under an ink-coloured sky a church keeps the soul from slumber. Rebuilding this church, atop this mountain, would be a reward for any traveller that finds it. Like climbing a peak.

Only pushing past roots, poisonous mushrooms, and brambles one discovers the strawberries, then the raspberries and the blueberries.

The Geoagiu Rotunda in Hunedoara County, dating from the 11th century, is the oldest ecclesiastical building still preserved in Romania. In many ways it is unique in the medieval religious architecture of this country.

According to tradition, this Romanesque chapel was built by the

Crusaders on their return from Jerusalem using bricks from *Germisara*, an old Roman fort located nearby. River stones were also used as building materials. Once belonging to the Akos family, it is currently the reformed church of the Hungarian community living here.

Romanian church porch.

45

Legendary First Saxons of Transylvania

They measured journey-time by the imminent birth of the babe who'd been but a thought when they'd left Hameln.

The clouds were dripping when, at last, word of lush pastures and springs was brought back by scouts. The land promised by the King!

The chieftains dropped to the ground, grass cushioning their knees. Bowing, Hermann smiled as birdsong covered the shriek of metal when they de-sheathed their swords.

Crossing them, they swore that their children's children will protect and love this country, in the Lord's name.

That Saxon's kin will prevail here till the swords' everlasting metal will become dust.

Transylvanian Saxons are people of German ethnicity who were first invited during the 12th century by King Géza II of Hungary to settle in Transylvania and defend the eastern border of his growing kingdom. The colonists were offered economical privileges.

The first Saxon immigrants settled in southern Transylvania where Sibiu County is today, while the existing inhabitants of the area were relocated. The territory conferred to them spread between Draas

(Drăuşeni) and Broos (Orăştie). It is said that on arrival the Saxon chieftains kneeled, crossed their swords, and swore that the undying metal of the two swords will foresee that their kin will live and last on this land forever. That only when the both swords will turn to dust, will the Saxon kin be gone. One sword was sent, and hidden, west in Broos city; the other one in east, in Draas. Only one sword was ever found.

Soon seven citadels of Transylvania, the Siebenburgen, blossomed: Bistriţa (then Bistritz), Braşov (Kronstadt), Cluj (Klausenburg), Mediaş (Mediasch), Sebes (Mühlbach), Sibiu (Hermannstadt) and Sighişoara (Schassburg). Some of these citadels even had their own judge and the right to apply capital punishment, unlike other Transylvanian settlements that were subordinated to a royal judge. This was something to be proud of and it was clear in the citadel's architecture: four turrets adorned the roof of the citadel's church tower.

So if you travel through Transylvania and spot four turrets, be on your best behaviour and know that you're in a village that once held the right of capital punishment.

Usually workshops were located inside the citadel towers so the craftsman had a double role: to produce according to their guild's craft in times of peace, and to protect the citadel in times of war.

Lutsch House, Sibiu

46

Unforgettable Legend of Râşnov's Coat of Arms

They were the first to arrive in Bursenland. A few men rode along a bouncy creek until they found their place; just right.

One climbed a hill, his sight sweeping all around. Mighty forests behind, plenty of wood, and a rare sight below: the valley was covered with flowering roses. It felt like home.

'If we settle here,' he told his companions, 'let our village be called the Roses Valley, Rosenau. May we never forget our homeland.'

The fortress stands there today.

Râşnov's coat of arms still showcases three roses, a reminder of a dream that came true among roses.

Râşnov in Romanian, *Rosnovia* in Latin, *Rosenau* in German, *Ruusenaa* in Transylvanian Saxon dialect, *Barcarozsnyó* in Hungarian, is a town in Braşov County, Transylvania. Located near the Roman fort of Cumidava, *Râşnov* fortress was first raised, out of wood and earth, by the Teutonic Knights at the beginning of the 13th century.

The Teutonic Knights were a religious catholic order established in 12th century Palestine by German crusaders.

In 1211 King Andrew II of Hungary offers the Knights land in the Carpathian Mountains, at the east border of Transylvania, loosely where Brasov County is found today. It was *Ţara Bârsei,* Burzenland or Terra Borza, named after the Cuman tribe Burci. The king planned to settle the Teutonic Knights in the area so they will defend Transylvania against the Cumans and the Pecheneg tribes that kept attacking. When, in 1224, the Teutonic Knights receive the approval of Pope Honorius III to create a state within a state, the Hungarian royal army came and attacked the Knights, who retreated in their wooden fortress, *Kreuzburg.* As it turned out, the Knights took more land than the king had gifted them initially. They were driven away in 1225.

Afterwards the Saxons already settled in Sibiu received new territories, namely Burzenland.

The river in the story is *Ghimbăşel* or Ghimbav, a tributary of Bârsa River that runs through Braşov.

Râşnov Fortress

47

The Screaming Waterfall, Buzaielor Country

Her nose was not crooked and there were no warts on her face. Her voice didn't crackle and she didn't own a black cat.

Thus, it took the villagers a long time to understand that the wickedness that had befallen upon them, one at a time, was her doing. Here a fall, there an upset stomach, a broken marriage, a sudden death, hail and locusts.

How happy were they to be rid of her!

But when the falling water sounded like a scream, they knew that it was the witch's voice, still haunting the land around the waterfall, The Holler.

Buzaielor Country on the curb of the Carpathians Mountains, southwest of Transylvania, was first documented during the 13th century as the Fortress of the Cross *(Kreuz Burg* in German, *Cetatea Crucii* in Romanian).

This fortress was built by the Order of the Teutonic Knights at *Tabla Buţii* Pass, or Tatar's Pass, an ancient road in Tatar Mountains, and was used as a defensive bastion and border custom point between Transylvania and Wallachia. After 1699, when Transylvania came under the rule of the Habsburg Empire, the customs' office was moved lower on Buzau River. The merchants who stopped here helped develop the town of Buzau.

Old border at Tatar's Pass.

48

Kronstadt, the Crown Burg, Brasov, a Hungarian Legend

King Solomon dug his heels into the flanks of his horse, leading his army further and further away from the Cuman invaders.

He needn't glance behind; arrows still rained over them no matter where he stirred his horse. Like a swarm of angry bees chasing a blob of golden honey, the Cumans followed. How could they?

His crown! The tell-tale sign! The king threw it aside, his men's lives coming first.

Years later, when the Saxons settled here, they found a tree and a crown lodged in it.

Honouring the memory of a passing king they called the town Kronstadt.

Braşov in Romanian, *Corona* in Latin, *Kronstadt* in German, *Kruhnen* in Transylvanian Saxon, *Brassó* in Hungarian, is a major city in Transylvania. The oldest human traces date back to the Neolithic period. Once it was the centre of Burzenland, and a significant commercial hub on the trade roads between Austria and Turkey. It was also the place where the national anthem of Romania was first sung.

After the crusaders were evicted the Saxon colonists and the local population formed the three settlements that will one day merge to form the city of Braşov: Corona, around the Black Church; Martinsberg, west of Cetăţuia Hill; and Bartholomä, on the eastern side of Sprenghi Hill.

View over Braşov and the Black Church.

49

Victorious Escape, Saint Ladislau at Calata Country, a Hungarian Legend

Only the years spent on horseback and the recent victory against plundering Cumans held Ladislaus on his mare. Beast and master, overcome by battle fever.

Yet victory was worthy. Each time.

A disturbance in the foliage; his ear picked up distress. A maiden, taken by a lost Cuman intruder! Ladislaus stirred his stallion into full pursuit, over hills, valleys, never catching-up.

He hurried the girl to push the Cuman off.

Throwing himself over the kidnaper Ladislaus fought till midnight. When the girl cut off the Cuman's leg and Ladislaus won.

One should never be picky when it comes to allies.

Țara Călatei in Romanian, *Kalotaszeg* in Hungarian, The Land of Călata, is situated west of Cluj-Napoca, western Transylvania, and is centred on Huedin town.

Ladislaus I, also known as Saint Ladislas, was King of Hungary from 1077 and King of Croatia from 1091. Today the Roman Catholic Church considers St. Ladislaus as the patron saint of Transylvania.

Evangelic Church, Bistrița

50

Ursula and the Gothic Knight from Bistrița Fortress

Connected to this eastern earth by way of horseback, they've arrived chasing dreams of a better life and a Hungarian King's promise if they settled, protected, and thrived on the furthest border of HIS still expanding new kingdom.

But now, with the echoes of Tatar horses gone, aiming for the heart of the continent, gone were the fruits of their labour. Burned. Pillaged. Killed. Without a prosperous life to show for themselves, Nösen on Bistrița will never be free; nor hold an annual fair, nor appear on a map.

Unless, unless a woman shared her riches with them, unlucky dreamers.

The Saxons who settled in southeast, where they discovered an old Roman castra, formed Burzenland (with towns such as Bran, Brasov, Prejmer); the settlers who moved to the northeast of Transylvania formed Nösnerland, with towns along Bistrița and Mureș Rivers. Here, Nösen on Bistrița was founded 1206, later known as Bistritz, and today as Bistrița.

51

Towering at Cârta Monastery, a Saxon Legend

When monks started laying stone upon stone, raising their monastery's walls like an immortal prayer to God, the devil squirmed underground.

Envious. Throwing rocks, piling them… downwards; upside-down towers pointing towards hellish fires.

Above, monks worked under the blessed light of sun. Smiling. Raising a church where all could pray to God.

Underneath, *belzebut* cursed, rattling the earth above, building a mightier edifice where, surely, more would want to come and sing his praises.

One night, the monks built a dam on Olt River flooding the land beneath. Today, Cârța Monastery still stands. The swamp nearby is feared by all.

Somewhere in wonderful Transylvania, in Făgăraş County, about 50 km from Sibiu when heading towards Braşov, you will discover a strange place with a wicked fame: Cârța Monstery.

During the 12th century the Cistercian Monks built two monastic ensembles in Romania; one in Timiş, completely destroyed today.

The second one was at Cârța. It is said that the monks who lived here had such a tough life that they died early, too early, and that when the monastery was built the devil competed in building its own place of worship, underneath. Besides the history of this place, besides its legends, remains the strange feeling all Cârța visitors have, that someone watches them all the time, and that this place hides a really dark mystery.

52

Up at Bran, Building a Stronghold

Once upon a time, and this is a true story, a mighty stronghold rose in the blink of an eye. A King, Louis I of Anjou, gifted to Brasov's inhabitants the green mountainous land at Bran Pass.

Because they "freely and in good will, generously and unanimously promised to build a new stronghold in Bran, by themselves, by their own work, by their own money, and clear the wood around," along and across the hills and deep into the valleys.

From there to oversee the enemy's potential penetration; the Hungarians' enemy; the Saxon's enemy, and the Romanians' enemy.

The Yatagan.

In 1377 (one century after the Teutonic Knights were chased away from Burzenland) Hungarian King Louis I of Anjou issued a document granting the people of Brasov the right to build a stone fortress at Bran. The wooden fortress Dietrichstein built here by the Teutonic Knights had collapsed during the Mongol rides of 13th century.

The rise of the Ottoman Empire started in 1299 when Prince Osman I founded it. The Yatagan was a threat for Eastern and Central Europe until its decline in the 17th century.

Romania, Serbia and Bulgaria declared their independence from the Ottoman Empire only in 1878.

53

Soimos Fortress, a Hawk's Nest in Lipova, Crisana

Snowflakes held time at ransom.

Amid the white vista, a mould. Perched on it, the goshawk. Eyes closed; heart pounding; crowned by the yellow marking on his beak. Snowflakes held their breath; the stillness after a snow-storm.

Then it happened: another heartbeat throbbed through the frozen earth. Long ears. As the rabbit leaped, so did the goshawk, his wings as silent as the fallen snow.

The bunny jumped. A shadow loomed over snow. Long ears laid low. Deadly talons locked as lethal as the icy ground. Bird and prey, returned to the mound: the man.

Who was the hunter now?

Perched on a cliff named The Slovak's Mountaintop, *Cioaca Tăutului*, the Hauk Fortress, *Şoimoş,* was raised during the 13th century to withstand the Tatar invasions. It is located on the perimeter of idyllic Lipova City, Arad County, in Crişana.

Şoimoş Fortress, up on a hill.

54

Right on Time, the Sighisoara Clock

For millennia, the green basins and white peaks of Carpathian Mountains were a harsh and uncompromising environment. Yet shepherds dotted their crests with snowy sheep, and villagers found refuge in the arms of their forests during wearying invasions.

Often and from far away hungry troops, armed troops, disturbed their meadows and their stony peaks for salt, iron, and gold!

Yet what is a land without unwavering folk?

Here, on a hill sung to sleep by the Târnava River, this landscape forged its first watchmakers. Building upon past generation's resourcefulness they invented complex mechanisms capable of decoding the mysteries of fleeting-time.

Sighişoara in Romanian, *Segesvár* in Hungarian,: *Schäßburg* in German, *Schäsbrich* in Transylvanian Saxon, *Castrum Sex* (six-sided camp) in Latin, is the only medieval fortress in southeast Europe that is still inhabited, and a city on the Târnava Mare River in Mureş County, Transylvania.

Sighisoara's Clock Tower that was built in the 13th century is the main entry point in the old medieval fortress.

Its first clock, built out of wood, dates from 1604 and was one of the first of its time. In 1648 the watchmaker Johann Kirchel, married to a local girl, installed the minute hand on the clock.

55

The Legend in the Tower, Densuş Church

When the sun smiled
Girls came by,
With her wedding cloth,
Flowers for her oath,
Old crown for her head,
Dull beads for her neck,
Rotten wood and shells.
Stale neckband of coins,
The price of her loins.
Dazed, Zanfira smiled
The tower she climbed,
Dressed in pure white robe,
Bare feet on cold stone,
All her pain locked tight
But her heart alight
Full of want for one,
Young love of her life
Poor, without a hide
To pay for a bride.
Beat up to death,
She'll meet in a breath.
Alas, he came' round, torn,
Zanfira to mourn.

Densuş Church (also known as St Nicholas' Church) in Densuş village, Hunedoara County, is one of the oldest stone churches in Romania. It was built during the 13th century in its present form, on the site of a 2nd-century Roman temple, with stones brought from the Dacian Sarmizegetusa Fortress.

'Saint Nicholas' Church, Densuş

56

The Maramures Gates

Carved from oak chopped under full-moon, the Maramueş Gates whisper stories that can be grasped with the eyes and the hands.

Our present lives draw from our past and spill into the future like the tree of life blessed by the cross.

Stay unyielding, honest, and whole like a rope made of one piece, and as clean as a fish that glistens in a mountain spring.

Life's a blessing under the sun, and abundant it can be, although it is a binding of good and evil, light and darkness.

Fastened only with treenails, not iron, the Maramueş Gates live forever.

The Maramureş Gates are one of the most precious symbols of Maramureş Country. Built out of oak or sessile wood and standing on three pillars, the gates have a girder beam and, above it, a roof covered with shingles. Often, the Maramureş Gates have been compared to triumphal arches. Maybe because for local peasants passing under such a gate is a ceremonial act, the man mentally purifying himself of the evils of profane world he came from, in order to enter cleanly into the domestic universe of his household and his family. In all traditional cultures the passage under a gate, more or less grandiose, symbolizes a transformation.

Many historians claim that, in Maramureş, the gates were a privilege of the *nemeş* (a local, richer family). The peasant families could only afford a gate of smaller proportions and with less woodwork called *vraniţa.*

Maramureş Gates, detail

57

A White Lie on the Lie Bridge in Sibiu

The hen strutted, her head popping forward to the rhythm of her scrawny feet. As queen of the yard, each bug was hers. A white queen, her feathers bright in the morning sun.

'Such a shame,' thought the woman as she grabbed the bird by the neck. 'And the last to survive her brood, too. After a spring drenched in dry spells, we've no wheat, nor worms to feed these birds.'

Dipping the hen in walnut dye, the woman smiled.

'Market day tomorrow.'

For a black hen one paid less tax.

'If only the bridge will hold my white lie.'

Because this bridge found in beautiful Sibiu was not built on pillars, it was called *Liegenbrücke* in German, which means 'lying bridge'. This name is almost homophonous to *Lügenbrücke*, 'the lie bridge', which is why some locals started calling it the 'bridge of lies' and thus many legends that justified its nickname were born.

The controversial bridge of Sibiu.

58

The Girls' Fair in Zarand Country

On the first Saturday after Saint John's Feast bakers from Alba County set off in carts loaded with honey cakes and bottles of mead to the top of Găina Mountain.

To the fair.

A cheerful gathering will soon be merry, dance, sing, and admire the girls' dotting. Golden and silvery plates, embroidered cloths, cushions, dowry chests, all loaded in horse-drawn carriages and brought to show.

The sound of the *tulnic* welcomes them. It once announced distress, danger, it sent villagers fleeing into hiding; today it brings them atop Găina Mountain, Hen's Mountain, singing a happy rhythm.

'Tis the Girls' Fair.

Zarand Country is located on the west side of the gentle slopes of Apuseni Mountains, along the banks of White Criş River.

Today the tradition of the Girls' Fair on Hen Mountain has travelled the world. One of the authors of the most impressive descriptions of the holiday was the writer Jokai Mor, at the end of the 19th century:

"On the evening of the first Saturday after the feast of the birth of Saint John, in Sânziene, the turtlers from Băiţa and Câmpeni, with their horses loaded with honey cakes, with bottles full of mead, set off for the top of Găina mountain, where they set up tents, and during the day next, the cheerful population gathers at the girls' fair that is being held that day on the top of the peak."

Girls playing the tulnic (bicium in Romanian).

59

Dipşa's Sow Church, Where Pigs Fly

13th was their century, their time to live and stay alive during hammering Tatar invasions. Always prepared. Not by fighting back, it got others killed, but, like birds, fleeing for their lives.

They gathered their most precious belongings: few glass beads, a gold coin saved over a lifetime of hard labour, a ring with a stone, small, meaningful treasures, and hid them in a caldron. That, they carried and buried. Together.

Till better times.

Till pigs will fly.

Peace came two centuries later. Then, they say, a sow never stopped rummaging till she found the buried treasure from the legend.

The Evangelical Church of Dipşa (Bistriţa-Năsăud County, northern Transylvania), was built at the end of the 15th century. Initially Catholic with the conversion of the German-born population to Lutheranism during the 16th century the church became evangelical. After the exodus of the Transylvanian Saxons the church was bought by the Orthodox community.

On one of the frontispieces there is a bas-relief of the sow who, according to the legend, found the treasure that used to build this place of worship, known today as the “Sow’s Church”.

The statue of a sow on Dipşa Church.

60

Vein Victims of Transylvania's Tallest Tower, Bistriţa or Sibiu?

The whole town was in the square. Builders, carpenters, ironsmith; the bellied Mayor; the cassocked priest; mothers cradling babes and young'uns between their skirts. Cats. Dogs.

Sibiu's will be 'the grandest tower of all Siebenbürgen,' the Mayor proclaimed. Hats fell, eyes lifted skywards where their tower will end.

'And Bistriza's tower?' The Mayor darkened. 'Build a taller one!'

Two sneaked in at night, climbed Bistriza's tower, dropped rope and measured. Hard work got 'em thirsty. Tzuica proved good at loosening tongues.

Sibiu's tower rose 2 meters short. Same 2 meters that were cut from the rope of two drunken men.

The steeple of the Lutheran Cathedral of Saint Mary in Sibiu is 73 meters tall; the tower of the Evangelical Church in neighbouring Bistriţa rises as 75 meters, making it the highest medieval tower in Romania.

Tzuica, *ţuică*, is a strong traditional Romanian spirit drink.

61

The Value of Hunyadi's Ring

Legend says that King Sigismund of Luxemburg and Hungary succumbed to the charm of Elizabeth, a fair maiden from Haţeg.

Alas, the King was married.

As to not dishonour her, the King married her to Knight Voicu. Then gifted her unborn babe a ring, to later recognize him by.

When the lad, Hunyadi, was the height of a sapling, a raven attracted by lustre stole the ring. The boy shot an arrow that caught the raven in mid-flight.

On hearing such tale the King was mighty impressed, bestowing Hunyadi a raven with a ring in its beak as family crest.

John Hunyadi was one of the greatest military commanders of the Middle Ages. His mother was Erzsébet Morzsinai; his father was Voicu, a Wallachian boyar who served in the army of Sigismund of Luxembourg, King of Hungary and Holy Roman Emperor.

The son of John Hunyadi to Erzsébet Szilágyi was Matthias Corvinus, born in Cluj, who became King of Hungary in 1458. He reigned for 32 years until his death, remembered as one of the greatest Hungarian kings.

Hunyadi Coat of Arms visible on the tympanum of this Corvin Castle door.

62

Witchcraft or Death Organ at Prejmer

The fortress rose on walls four meters thick, twelve meters high, fortifications reinforced under King Sigismund of Luxemburg.

For defence, hot oils were poured through attack holes; arrows spitted before any Turkish invaders even approached the wide moat. Anything, everything to protect the church, their faith, nestled inside.

But their main defence weapon was the death organ. Its sounds, once leaving the shell of the fortress, would coil, rise to such piercing heights, and drop to such hollowed depths that the effect, physically unbearable, petrified any invader from inside out.

It was nicknamed the unbreakable fortress.

Untouchable over fifty times.

Prejmer Fortress is located 15km from Braşov, near Buzau Pass. The church was founded in the 13th century by the Germanic Teutonic Knights. It was nicknamed the *Unvanquishable* because the Ottomans tried to conquer it fifty times, and fifty times they failed. This happened after 'The Death Organ', a deadly fighting device, arrived at Prejmer. The sounds it produced scared off any attackers. The Turks were so frightening by them that they no longer dared approach this stronghold.

Prejmer Fortress.

63

He Was Vlad the Impaler

Until it perishes under Saint Michael's lance a Dragon cannot die. It sleeps.

Till it awakens.

Some only heard of his deeds from stories filled with his doings, the Impaler's. These fashioned their own image of him, one that suited THEM. No one else would have been as daring as he.

Those who'd met him asked themselves if what they've met was made of flesh, or mere spirit.

What lingered in everyone's mind was his strength. His will.

The make of a hero.

Fighter. Killer. Lover. But mostly fighter. In the front line.

For his kin. For Balkans.

For Europe.

Vlad III, known as Vlad the Impaler or Vlad *Drăculea,* was born in 1431 in Sighişoara. The house where he was born still stands today.

He was the second son of Vlad II Voivode of Wallachia also known as Vlad *Dracul* after his induction into the Order of the Dragon that was created by Holy Roman Emperor Sigismund to defend Christian Europe against the Ottoman Empire.

Vlad tee Impaler was the grandson of Mircea the Elder, a valiant and long-time ruling Voivode of Wallachia, 32 years, an extended time for that era, and cousin to Stephen the Great of Moldova.

In Romanian language dragon and dracul (devil) are similar sounding words. *Dracul-a* (as Vlad III was named) meaning son of Dracul (Vlad II).

Throughout his childhood and the years spent at the Ottoman court (under Sultan Murad II) as hostage to secure his father's loyalty, Vlad III was exposed to German, Hungarian, and Ottoman cultures and leadership styles. In addition, he also spoke Latin and Romanian and even some Slavonic. At the Ottoman court Vlad III became acquainted with the Turkish war tactics and tortures, skills he later used in battles against ottomans.

Vlad fought all his life to regain the throne of Wallachia. He succeeded in ruling his father and grandfather's country on three occasions, as Wallachia had no rule of primogeniture thus the throne was not passed from father to son under the law.

During his battles for the throne of Wallachia and then as its Voivode fighting the Ottoman troops but also the Hungarians rulers (both powers wishing to secure their influence over Wallachia, a country that stood between them as a buffer zone), Vlad the Impaler gained many enemies. Adding to this the plots involving Wallachian nobles and those of John Hunyadi, regent-governor of Hungary, Vlad only secured his father's seat for seven years. One last plot proved fatal and he was killed in battle.

His legacy outlasted many others. Primary and secondary sources depict Vlad the Impaler as an unforgettable ruler, "a man of unheard cruelty and justice" (Antonio Bonfini). But the realities of his times should be considered too. The way Europe perceived his country, Wallachia, as a dispensable, weak pawn, and how only he could demand respect for it, as its Voivode, through the image he projected and through his deeds (on or outside the battlefield).

Sighişoara: the house where Vlad the Impaler was born (yellow, on right hand side)

64

The Arrival of Autumn

On the hip of the hill the grass ripens. Spring's shamrock changed its coat for a lustre-less pickle that turns to mulch through rainfalls.

Ahead, among the fruity shade, I spot bunches of ripen apples smiling a blushing red. I step in their cool shade, among grass blades up to my hip, and quench my thirst on ripen fruit.

The grass sings with the breeze, letting go, unconcerned, of what must change.

Among old, dry blades, I spot new shoots.

I stand and face life again, greedy for this new chance at what sipped through my fingers, with summer's heat.

From valleys to the woodlands, autumn has arrived.

65

The Woodland

It's known as a dark land where a blood-thirsty vampire, Vlad the Impaler, still haunts, condemned to drag his immortality to the threshold between history and legend.

It reveals itself as a land of passionate people, proud of their ancestry, yet a land torn between them. An apple of discord.

Ravaged through *falx*, sword and *yatagans*, sought-after by emperors, voivodes, sultans, the Land-Beyond-the-Forest has been freed one more time than it's been conquered.

The life of its people was intertwined with the vigour of forests. Hiding inside from invaders; building, burning down, then rebuilding wooden churches, hopes after each war.

66

Victims on Foot, Jewish Emigrants to Transylvania

The cold rain hit their wind-weathered faces. Their hunched backs carried parcels stuffed with only the bare necessities for a long journey eastwards.

Every day, a different landscape.

Their home was sometimes wide plains; other times plaintive forests. Their nights were invigorated by huge bonfires and lit by bright stars. Their food could be any fruit they found along the way; flat bread baked by a fire.

All they had were memories of a bygone era, of angry, confined, dark cities to which they'd never return.

The new nomads travelled searching for a free life.

Hope was a stern mistress.

During the 1348 - 1351 outbreak of Black Death in Europe the Jewish communities were falsely blamed. Mass persecutions and massacres started in Provence in April 1348, then in Barcelona. In 1349 the hatred wave (together with the plague) reached Erfurt, Basel, Aragon, Flanders, and Berne. Here, the citizens compelled the city council to take an oath that they will burn the Jews and interdict any

Jew to enter their city for the next two hundred years. The city deputies said that they knew no evil in the Jews. They were promptly deposed and the new council gave in to the mob, arresting the Jews on Friday, the 13th. The hatred culminated with the Valentine's Day massacre from Strasbourg. Those Jewish families that could, emigrated eastwards to the Hungarian Kingdom. Where the hatred reached them yet again.

Before fleeing Hungary they were only allowed one job, to collect money. And who likes the tax collector? And the debt collector? No one! Everyone held a grudge against them. The Hungarian Kingdom expelled them because the King wanted to increase his political power and was searching for a scapegoat. He expelled the Jews (after he confiscated their lands) on the note that their presence was a state within a state and thus endangered the safety of his kingdom.

The Jewish families arrived in Transylvania. Some went further north to Russia, some even further, to Ukraine.

The Synagogue of Brasov.

67

In Love all Things Seem Possible

Under night's velvet cover Voyk slid along the turret taking most of the climbing rose down with him. He stifled a whimper as his bare feet, who'd collected most thorns, hit the cobbled yard.

A roar of anger echoed from the room above as Enyko's father, sword in hand, half-bent over the window promised a death not even a soldier as experienced as Voyk had ever heard of.

All because of his Vlach heart, who'd fallen under the spell of a Hungarian maiden.

Voyk backed out, sorrow he kicked off his boots so eagerly. Happy his trousers were still on.

During Transylvania's tumultuous medieval history interracial relations were discouraged. Hungarians, Saxons, Szeklers, and Vlachs (local Romanians) all had to keep to their clans. While the Catholic and Orthodox worshipers were prohibited to marry one another.

68

Keep Nature as a Gift

Mountains that watch over a timeless land, once lone guardians now tender lovers.

Rivers that come and go through eternity, washing away pain, blood spilled in battles, and replenishing hope.

Plains as peaceful as a sleeping maiden awaiting the last kiss of the moon, and the first sight of the sun.

Unblemished flowers looking up, praying to the same God, their roots anchored in the earth of their ancestors.

Never ours, nor theirs to keep. But our children's, and their children's children.

This land is our history, our wealth, and knowing it is like knowing our parents.

An everlasting gift.

69

Head to Poiana Brasov, to the Church of Pagans

When wild men haunted these forests an ancient pagan temple rose here. Later, the forest people disappeared but the stone slab remained, empty offering to the stars.

During one of the numerous sieges on Râşnov some Turkish soldiers got lost in these forests, during a hasty retreat. Because they were afraid to fall into the hands of the brave warriors of Ţara Bârsei, they hid in a cave and remained hidden for a long while, using a fitting stone table for their ritual offerings.

You can still spot it today, at The Church of Pagans, if you climb to Poiana.

It is only a rock, a solitary spot in the middle of a sea of tranquillity, but if you listen to legends you understand that the surrounding peace is only the breeze of a millennial serenity bought by countless prayers still suspended in the air around.

The Pagan's Church in autumn.

70

Grind and Grime of a Janissary

The Janissary pressed his face against the cold, rough stone. His fingers, shaking, dug deeper into the fort's crevices. Steam billowed from his mouth. If he could have seen it, he'd have thought it was his soul, leaving his body.

'No prisoners!' *ağa* had ordered.

Hissing, he heaved himself loathing his heavy *yatagan*. But obeying orders meant living another day.

Then down went the blade, again and again

He'd saddled the wall back when it suddenly rained with arrows. One with the stone he counted ten floating bodies pulling crossbows!

The moonless night only allowed enough space for hopeless prayer.

Janissaries were the elite infantry troops closely guarding the Sultan and the first modern standing army (having a salary) in Europe. They became the avant-guard of the Ottoman troops. They were commanded by an *ağa,* fought with a Turkish sword, *yatagan,* and a weapon.

The ruins of Cuiesti Fortress are found on top of the hill known as the Turk's Lip, near Bocşa town, Caraș-Severin County, Banat.

It was the smallest in a row of fortresses and the one that the Turks battled to conquer. It went under siege in 1695. It is said that, when the Turks discovered that only a handful of Romanians had given them grief, they decapitated all the prisoners. That night, as legend goes, it rained with fire arrows over the sleepy Ottoman camp. Arrows shot by the floating bodies of the ten head-less, executed prisoners.

The ruins of Cuieşti Fortress.

71

Now, the Boy from the Big House and the Boy from the Barn

. . . Were of equal height under the summer sky, equally sun-burned.

The fruits never ripened with them around, the only difference that, for such sin, one was never punished while one received double payment across his back.

Only the time passed equally over them.

When war came, one went to lead his father's army. The other stayed behind to plow fields, dig trenches. Because of his lame shoulder, from all the beatings received as a child.

He dug graves too. One especially, that he worked the hardest for, wetting the earth with tears.

For the young hero from the big house...

72

A Prisoner of Her Time

She woke to a soft creaking.

The dizziness came as soon as she opened her eyes to darkness.

An ache in her shoulders told her she must be alive, yet she couldn't feel her arms. Eyes shut or not, her throbbing ankles told her she was hanging upside down.

Above, that creaking sound again. And drafts of air. As is something opened to the outside world, then closed again. A shuffling noise.

Light flickered outside her closed eyelids. Something sharp hissed above.

'Women can't be warriors," she heard before her body was freed and she dropped against rocks.

Head first.

Among the legacies of history past was the view that women were subordinated to men. The middle ages were perceived, and still are, as a male-dominated era. Still, many were those women who, through clever manipulation, managed to secure a seat of honour and power, rising above men's laws and even those of religion, taking a forefront seat in society and public life.

Feminism as an ideology and movement was a social phenomenon that dominated the society of the nineteenth century, originating in the 1848 Revolution along with other major phenomena such as national liberation movements, socialism, the labour movement, etc.

One of the first women movements in Transylvania was the philanthropic initiative of the women of Brasov. 'The Union of the Women of Brasov' was founded on 24 March 1850.

A Romanian pottery artist.

73

The Leaning Tower of Medias

In the city with four corner towers, illustrating its honour to apply the capital punishment, the Stonemason's Guild, ambitious, vowed to raise a fifth. To rival Vienna's Saint Stephen's Cathedral, the tallest steeple of Holy Roman Empire.

They set stone upon stone and, soon, the tallest tower rose; golden in the twilight.

And askew. Leaning through hasty work. The builders tore the hairs off their heads. Threw ropes around it, eager to fix their mistake before the mortar set and everyone noticed.

If only all pulled!

One, hands on the rope, had his eyes cast upon a maiden strolling by.

Mediaş in Romanian, *Medgyes* in Hungarian, *Medwesch* in Transylvanian Saxon, *Mediasch* in German is the second largest city in Sibiu County, after Sibiu.With signs of human settlements dating to Neolithic era, *Mediaş* is one of the cities developed by the Saxon settlers during the 13th century. The Trumpeters' Tower, built on the ruins of a Roman basilica belongs to St. Margaret Evangelical Church.

It received its name because guards would climb it and search the horizon for signs of danger such as fire outbreak or invasion. They would blow their trumpet to sound an alarm, warning the inhabitants.

The tower of the Evangelic Church.

74

Sentenced to the Lovers' Jail in Biertan

The people of Biertan lined up shoulder to shoulder, even children filling up the gaps between trousers and skirts. A narrow, silent corridor of flesh pointed towards the seventh tower of their fortress.

The jail.

There was no shaming. They spat no words of anger to the convicted couple struggling along the narrow path. To meet their faith.

'All things last but once. For your quarrelling, you are sentenced to sharing one single bed, one pillow, one table, one chair, one plate, one spoon, and one fork.'

There was no way out of the lover's tower, but hand in hand.

Biertan in Romanian, *Bierthälm* in German, *Berethalom* in Hungarian) was one of the first Transylvanian Saxon villages with a fortified church. First documented in 1224, Biertan is located in Sibiu County. Because the area was too often under threat from Tatar and Ottoman invasion Saxons built fortified communities with fortified churches. Reinforced with defence and storage towers, the fortified churches allowed Saxons to fight back and keep safe their most valuable goods, thus withstanding strenuous sieges.

Biertan was the seat of Saxon Episcopal Church for three centuries, between 1572-1867. Transylvania has many Saxon villages and even one Székely village with such fortified churches.

The Lover's Jail in Biertan is real while its fortress, built with the money and by the hands of its inhabitants, was conquered only once in over 500 years.

Biertan fortified church.

75

Haunted Legend at Banffy Castle

It was a child's play to kick leaves and poke holes with a stick. That's how they found the tunnel, or perhaps the tunnel allowed them that.

Cool, wider than any cave they knew, the tunnel even had tracks and a wagon the children pushed between the derelict castle and the church.

That year winter came early. But right before the snowfall, when the boys braved the night and entered the tunnel, a colony of bats detached itself from its walls and swooped towards them.

After that, everyone said the tunnel was haunted. They closed it.

Now it's waiting. Again.

Between 1437 and 1543 the Banffy family built near Small Someş River a castle with four towers. They lived there until 1944 when they were evacuated by the Germans who wanted to turn the castle into a military WW2 hospital. It is the largest castle in Transylvania built in Baroque style, also known as the Versailles of Transylvania or Electric Castle. Banffy Castle is considered to be one of the most haunted places in Romania.

76

Shepherding, a Life Enough

'PHWEEEE!' The shepherd whistles and in the distance the herding dogs stir the sheep.

'WHOA!' The old man snorts as he walks hunchbacked, like an old crooked tree, into the wind.

'PHOOWEET!' And the shepherd, rod on his shoulder, leads along the road back home, home to a leaking roof, creaky floors, each step closer to his old woman, children, and love.

'WHOOEE-UUEET!' The wind pushes him faster along the trees planted by his lads, with a swing waiting for grandchildren, alongside the horse and lambs.

'PHWEEEE!' The man longs again for the fields, the bales, the weather. His freedom.

77

Shepherding, from Dobruja to Transylvania

Once a shepherd from Dobruja planned on travelling over Bucegi Mountains, towards prime pastures.

When he arrived at the foot of the mountain he fed his sheep and gave his dogs rest. Yet the beasts were restless, sniffing the air they once knew. And the shepherd found that his foot, too, remembered the hard path of his childhood, so different from the sandy, soft Dobruja.

His heart leaped when they reached the small village on the mountain's saddle.

With a bit of luck he'll make it over the mountain before Saint George's Day.

To the land where he'd been born.

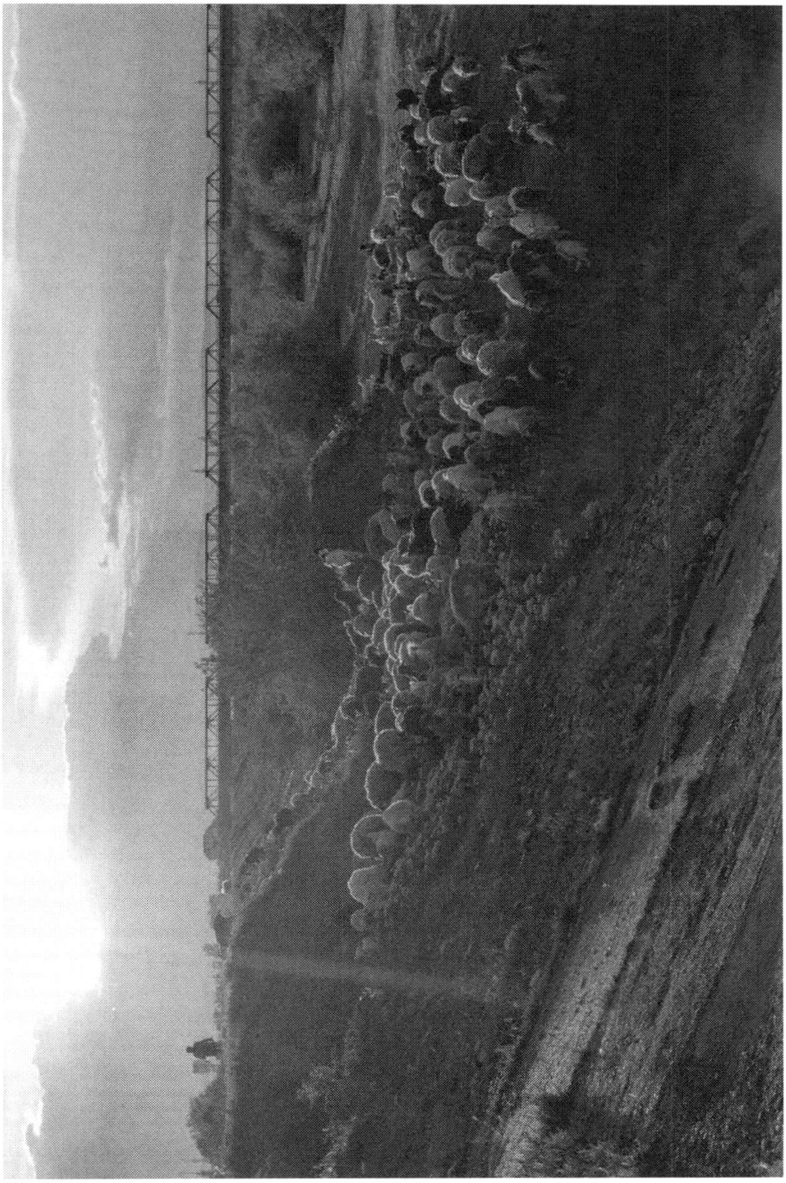

Shepherding, a lifestyle for few, a choice for all.

78

Under the Spell of a Healer in Miklósvár, Covasna

Icicles hung from braches. The world was frozen in silence through the frosted window.

the boy thought he was dreaming, losing the battle against his heavy eyelids. He shivered by a crackling fire, underneath two blankets.

By the rings under his mother's eyes, he'd been sleepwalking again. She must have kept him from strolling into the icy night.

A horseshoe stomping behind a curtain marked time.

Auntie grunted, stirring lead in an iron pot. She eyed the cooling shape, her mouth moving. Shrieks and animal gurgle came out. Chanting.

He'll place the lead under his pillow to stop the night-wonder.

Miklósvár in Hungarian, *Micloşoara* in Romanian, is a village in Covasna County, eastern Transylvania. First mentioned in 1211 as Castrum Sanct Nicolai it has seen Tatar invasions, its inhabitants lived through Reformation, while during the Communist rule its residents have known a government-enforced exile. With pastel-coloured cottages, its elderly inhabitants still rely on horse-drawn carts and wood, smoke drifting up from chimneys all year around.

79

Warrior Sava Brancovici, a Baptism of Faith

A drip-drip marked the time.

To the man collapsed in the dungeon it was the rhythm of his unrelenting faith, each Friday bringing another flogging witnessed by his flock.

Under Ottoman rule life had been unbearable. With a Calvinist monarch it became hell.

Until a baptism was requested.

A flicker of hope? Or was he dead and this was purgatory?

The stench of the party-room assaulted him. The sight of the babe, a DOG, confirmed it.

'Bring me two dishes,' he sighed. 'Green beans, my meal. And pork-chop, yours. Whose meal this babe will choose, that one shall baptize him.'

During 1683 Sava Brancovici, the Metropolitan Bishop of the Orthodox Romanians living in Transylvania, was accused of treason for: preaching in a faith different than that of Calvinist-ruled Transylvania (now included in the Hungarian Empire). Brancovici never lost his faith.

Alone in his damp and cold cell he survived by recalling the past years and praying for the land and the people he once served with faith.

The Wooden Church of Ineu, the town where Sara Brancovici (Simeon Branković) was born.

80

Zeitgeist of Monastic Life

If you make it through the forest you'll reach the village with the same name. High iron-gates will suddenly rise ahead of you.

To your left, a stone tower partially grounded by time and weather. Go around it. In front of you will appear the last foundation of the Good King. It has that specific roof, without towers.

Then, climbing some steep, awkward steps, you will finally see the monastery.

In the beginning the building functioned as a prison, then as orphanage for girls. Only much later it housed the lonely cells for the monks.

Its walls finally knowing peace.

81

Withstand in Faith, Sebeş Tower and the Monk's Hill

Battle roaring, horses neighing, wounded moaning rose like miasma from the battlefield's hell to his hilltop, keeping him awake at night.

In his youth, when Murad's *yeniceries* attacked, his people sought refuge behind the thick walls of their Sebeş fortress. The lucky ones were smoked to death in the tower. Others, enslaved.

Today, when snowy hair mocked his still young heart, he stayed put when Turks approached his hut. Warrior or wounded in need of shelter.

Instead, he recognized their leader, the Bey who'd set him free after his 20-year life as a Turkish slave.

'You're safe, Mustafa,' he smiled.

Sebeş in Romanian, *Mühlbach* in German, *Szászsebes* in Hungarian, *Melnbach* in Transylvanian Saxon dialect is a city in Alba County, southern Transylvania. First a rural settlement inhabited by Romanian villagers, in 1150 the Saxons settlers raised the fortress that has known many Tatar and Ottoman invasions. In 14th century it was the first city in Transylvania to be completely surrounded by masonry fortifications.

The tower of Evangelic Church in Sebeş.

82

Whipping Matthias the King

Cheering mingled with whistling while the snapping of a whip marked the rhythm of labour.
In the central square a poor commoner, drenched in sweat, wrestled a log as thick as the leather girdle encircling his waist. As heavy as a bull.

None stepped forward, but a lad.

Cheering followed the royal entourage the next day.

At the place in the square where the log lay, abandoned, the King bent and showed all the marking he'd made the day before, when dressed as a poor lad he, alone, had helped the convicted, the man who knew how to show restraint.

It is said that Matthias Corvinus, who became one of the greatest kings of Hungary, more than once entered the city of Cluj incognito, to see how commoners were treated.

83

The Prinslop Monastery as a Bequest from Lady Zamfira

Words whisper from a slab of red marble:

"The wretched body of Saphira, once beloved daughter of Prince Moise, lies here to rest; a pride to her father and her grandfather, after which Dacia still cries.

"As beloved wife of Keseriu, she closed his eyes in death. As wife to Nisowski, she showed the Wallachian earth the value of her kin.

"You, who reads this, know that Saphira was worthy of her Safire name."

After the death of her second husband Saphira found refuge at Prislop Monastery, that she had founded.

Between descending paths, she always picked the ascending one.

The story of Prislop Monastery in the Upper Silvaşu Parish is first related to Saint Nicodim of Tismana and to the Wallachian Voivode Mircea the Elder who raised a wooden church here during the 14th century. Lady Zamfira, Saphira, the daughter of Wallachian ruler Moise-Voda, son of Vladislav III, built a stone church during the 16th century on the grounds belonging to the Romanian nobles of Ciula clan.

84

Was it Worth It - a Salt Mine Story from Turda

Moise's heartbeat matched the trotting of his horse as they followed the metal road to the whole in the hillside. At the entrance the man paused, hugged his mare, and brushed the glossy mane bringing thanks that both could work.

One last glance at daylight committing the birdsong to memory.

Man and horse stepped into the black mouth of the salt mine. For the remainder of the day only his torch will be his sun, only the pounding of the hammer his tune.

Today Moise drags his feet guiding his blind horse by a make-shift harness.

Mining had its price.

Salina Turda (Romanian), *Tordai sóbánya* (Hungarian) is a salt mine in Turda area, the second largest city in Cluj County, northwest Romania. The first pages of Salina Turda's story were written during the Roman occupation of Dacia when the city (then *castrum*, a Roman fort) was named Potaissa. Potaissa was be a more common pronunciation of the Dacian name Patreuissa. The beginnings of salt mining as we understand it today happened during the 11th - 13th centuries.

Hungarian documents from 1075 and 1271 mention the Turda Salt Mine and its importance as main source of supplies for the region. During the 19th century the Turda Salt Mines became "so famous that they have almost no equal in the whole east" (Johann Fridwaldsky, mineralogist).

The workers in Turda Salt Mine were free men and the contract lasted only one year. Payment for the year was 12 (Hungarian) Florins, as well as holiday gifts (for Christmas, Easter, Pentecost and All Saints Day), namely a barrel of wine, an ox (exchangeable for 4 Florins), and 100 breads (exchangeable for two Florins).

Horses were used to move the pulleys that brought the salt to the surface. Sadly, the horses would go blind after only one week of work underground and become skinny in six months.

Salina Turda was included in '25 Unbelievable Travel Destinations You Never Knew Existed' by Business Insider in 2013.

Inside Salina Turda.

85

On the Trail of the White Gold, at Turda Salt Mines

Old folk speak of a maiden courted by many.

A Duke, richer than any, offered her a ring.

A date was set.

Yet the bride asked not for gold, silver or jewels as a dowry. Her future husband's wealth knew no measure.

She asked for something more precious instead.

White Gold.

Gathering his army, her father brought her to the only salt mine in their part of the world, at Turda. The girl knew they cannot move it to her land; nor could they take God's gift to others.

So she threw her engagement ring into the mine shaft instead.

86

Oldest and Tiniest, a Story for the Wooden Church of Doba

When Iliora was born the tree was as tall as a sapling, still wrestling the summer storms.

As Iliora grew the tree shot up, his branches touching the sky.

But when Iliora married and moved over the hill, the tree grew taller so he can keep an eye on his girl.

Then Iliora died.

Others cut down the tree. Built a church over the hill. Later, they moved it back, to fill an empty spot that was just right.

Legend says that the tree knew.

He'd known from the beginning that one day a church will stand in its place.

Any place has a story, any place deserves a story; this is the one for the oldest and tiniest wooden church from *Zona Codrului*, Woodland Realm, in Maramures, Romania. It is the late 16th century wooden church of Doba, dedicate to Archangels Michael and Gabriel.

Quiet, the Wooden Church of Doba.

87

Gazing at the Stars

The old man learned to mock the horrors of passing wars by observing the stars, harassing galaxies and quasars with the aid of a telescope or just from memory.

He made out the cratered surfaces of the moon, so quiet compared to the craters of war.

The grey desolation like a battle's aftermath.

Within reach, yet untouchable, like the ideal a war was started upon.

Those gazes into infinity imprinted a passion that helped him forget his earthly pains.

Although he spent years gazing upwards, he was only able to escape from this place on the day of his death.

88

Remote in Winter

The wind howls and hits the windows. The rain patters against the roof, usual music in my day to day life. The sound of crackling flames in the wood stove and their heat fills the room.

The cat meows lazily and stretches along the windowsill, ignoring the desolate landscape devoid of any green. A grey winter.

A lonesome snowflake hangs outside the glass.

The cat watches it.

Many people will come and go, finding this place beautiful once under snow. For me, this landscape and its climate are nothing new. They are part of my life.

I feel at home.

Holy Trinity Church reflected by a semi-frozen Târnava Mare River, Sighişoara.

89

Jewels, Wooden Churches from Chiesd, Salaj County

For the perfect oak, one naturally crooked to allow for slicing of curved planks, the carpenters searched into the depths of the forest. Where man never set foot and only the light of the sun and the song of bird touched it.

The church's apse, rounded like shoulders stooped in prayer, rose on sturdy beams joined without nails.

And then, by rolling it on wood stumps they moved it, taking as long as it was needed.

Two years.

Two years of Sunday service held wherever the church's transportation had paused.

The church built only of wood, of faith, and skill.

Sălaj County (or Land of Silvania, *silva*, meaning forest in Latin) is located in the northwest of Romania in historical province of Crişana.

It is a land that can be very proud of its unique wooden churches. The wooden church in Chieşd was built during the 18th century. Legend has it that it was originally built about 300 meters from its current site. It was moved on wooden logs, without being disassembled.

The whole operation took about two years during which time the mass was held at the place where the church was located for the day.

The Church of Chiesd.

90

The Hajduk

The *hajduk* stirred up his whip, the Hutzul went crazy arching his broad back, jumping across the path. The dust did not allow distinguishing between man and horse.

Dancing, united in fight, the rider clung as beastly as he could to the raging whirlwind.

Down the valley, the attackers released their first war-cry. The *hajduk* raised his fist proudly. The Hutzul sprang to freedom.

Soon, a church-bell will ring in warning. Villagers will hide for their lives.

They might not know who the *hajduk* was, but know he's out there: by the breeze that he stirs as he gallops away.

A *hajduk* was a Robin-Hood figure who lived in Transylvania during the 17th - 19th centuries. He was an outlaw, a thief, a highwayman, and a mercenary mostly taking from the rich (especially Turks, Hungarians, or Russians) and helping out the poor, the peasants. At the same time he would also defend the peasants against Cossack, Polish or Tatar attacks.

The Hutzul, *huţul*, *hucul* horse is small horse breed originally from the Carpathian Mountains. It has a calm and good disposition, with a heavy build and possesses great endurance and hardiness.

91

The Ballad of Pintea, Hajduk of Maramures

The mountain Pintea climbed,
Built yard painted white,
With broad sticks he fenced it,
With leaves he covered it.
Then Pintea called,
If there's one,
To Baia Mare stride,
After bread, salt, to ride,
And chilled red wine,
That boyars drink 'all time.

His brother-in-arms called:
I'll ride, Pinteo, I'll go
If you'd lend me your roan,
Your wind-fast home-grown.
But if the guard finds me,
Your death will weigh on me.
What shall your price be,
Tell, brother, save me.

Three grains of rye in wind,
Three of wheat in spring,
Three of holy wheat
A proud silver lead.

Cetatea Chioarului, Chioar Fortress, Kővár vára in Hungarian, is located in Maramureş, near Berchezoaia village. The fortress was raised to safeguard the road connecting Maramures to Transylvania. It is believed that it was built, from wood and earth, after the Mongol invasion of 1241. There are three legends related to Chioariului Fortress. According to the first legend Hajduk Pintea's outlaws took refuge here. The second legend reminds of a secret entrance, through a hidden tunnel located just below the fortress' stone walls. The third one mentions its fountain, said to never dry out due to its depth which is why the people call it "the bottomless fountain".

Pintea was a renowned Hajduk, a Robin Hood of Maramures, who lived especially Lăpuş Cuntry, Năsăud, and Chioarului Country. The biggest action related to the beginnings of his outlawry was the attack on Count of Rona's castle where 250 people had been known to be killed without any grounds. Consequently King Leopold I offered 500 imperial Thalers reward on Pintea's head. Pintea's Ballad is an outlaw song collected orally, depicting his bravery.

National costumes of Maramureş.

92

Joseph and the Weapons on Tarnava

Bethlen came again. Dad payed him our earnings and got a flogging in return. Bethlen loves to practice shooting behind the field. His hand doesn't shake when he fires.

Once he helped me practice. Took me to the corn field and made me shoot a straw man from afar. There, he also taught me how to cut meat. When I handed him the rabbit, he gave me a new bullet, smiling only with his mouth.

Later, at home, I examined the trophy. In his reflection I saw the straw-man, expressionless.

My hand did not shake when the Emperor stayed over.

Inhabited from the Paleolithic era all through the Roman occupation of Dacia and into the medieval period Dumbrăveni is located not far from Sighişoara and Mediaş, in Târnava County, central Transylvania.

Dumbrăveni was first mentioned in documents in the 14th century as Ebes. Less than two centuries later the village was deemed important enough that the Governor of Transylvania built here the Bethlen Castle. On 1st June 1773 Emperor Joseph II, while he still co-ruled with his mother Maria Theresa, visited Dumbrăveni (then one of the ten free cities of Transylvania) and spend the night at the local inn. The Emperor participated in the armed exercises of the Habsburg troops.

At that time the Romanian peasants were, more than often, *iobagi* (from Magyar *jobbágy*, tied to the land of a feudal master, belonging to him with their life and everything they owned). The *robota* (from Latin *rob/robie*, menaing slavery) binds the *iobagi* to the feudal ruler for life. *Iobagia* was first documented in Transylvania in 1291 and was abolished in 1848.

Red Lake

93

Into the Water, the Red Lake Legend up in Harghita

Once upon a time there lived a beautiful girl, Esther. Her hair like raven's feathers, eyes like emeralds, she was a flower swaying in the wind.

One sunny summer day Esther met a tall, handsome lad, stronger than a bear, his voice sweeter than birdsong. The lad gifted Esther a scarf and begged her to wait for his return from the army.

Only the mountain knew her longing.

When an outlaw abducted beautiful Esther the mountain heard and crumbled in aid. Burying her.

If you glance into the water of Red Lake, you can spot the gleam of Esther's eyes.

Red Lake (*Lacul Roșu* in Romanian, *Gyilkos-tó* or *Veres-tó* in Hungarian) is a natural dam lake in Hășmaș Mountains on the upper course of the Bicaz River, Harghita County. The lake formed following the collapse of a slope due to the earthquake of 23rd January 1838 that measured 6.9 magnitudes on the Richter scale.

94

Young and Old - When Avram Iancu Met the Emperor

When Iancu entered to see the Emperor, three candles burned in his hand and three other candles burned in the Emperor's hand. The candles before the Emperor went out by themselves.

Iancu stepped closer and lit the Emperor's candles. His did not extinguish. As soon as he retreated, however, the Emperor's candles went out but Iancu's candles remained lit. Again, Iancu lit the Emperor's candles.

'Iancu, my son,' said the old Emperor, 'I will not continue to oppose God anymore. I have now understood His will and I agree that from now on you will be the king of Transylvania.'

Avram Iancu (1824-1872) was a lawyer and military hero of Romanians living in Transylvania especially during the Revolution of 1848. Iancu's activities embodied the liberal and national aspirations characteristic of his generation. In March 1848, when he learned of the declaration of civil and political freedoms by Hungarian liberals of Pest, he joined his Hungarian colleagues in Tirgu-Mures hoping for a new era of fraternity and equality between Hungarians and Romanians. He also wished to gain recognition for Romanians as a nation equal to Hungarians and the other nations living in Transylvania (when part of Romanians living here were *iobagi*, serfs, forced to obey their Hungarian nobles).

Because so many held him in high regard, Avram Iancu's nickname was Crăişorul Munţilor, Prince of the Mountains.

Avram Iancu memorial house.

95

Time-lapse, Halmagiu Church, Arad

My feet carry me on a path like any other, nature reclaiming its own territory but under the overgrow I hear echoes of history.

I hear salt merchants whose donkeys, slow under the weight of white gold, have levelled it by trotting.

I hear Roman soldiers, whose sandals chanted in the fast rhythm of battle, marching along the same road, paved, to conquer richer lands.

I hear laughter and merriment as people became free, free to worship and live by their faith, and raise a marble church, to last. And I hear wailing, as humans are whipped into submission again.

Hălmagiu in Romanian, *Nagyhalmágy* in Hungarian, is a village in Arad County, west of Romania. The Orthodox Church of Hălmagiu, of the 'Dormition of the Virgin', is one of the testimonies of the medieval life of Romanians while Transylvania was integrated into the Hungarian Kingdom.

While vestiges of Roman roads were discovered nearby (roads once used by salt merchants) as well as marble Byzantine ruins, 11th-century chronicles mention here the Duchy of Prince Menumorut, local Romanian ruler at the time of Hungarian conquest of Transylvania.

The oldest votive inscription in the church suggests that it was built around 1400. During the 18th century the peasants who lived here and refused to convert to Catholicism were beaten at the stake in the same churchyard.

The Christin Orthodox Church from Hălmagiu

96

19th century Travels to Deva Fortress

I've travelled the world but I've never seen a mountain as majestic as the one near Deva, crowned by grand ruins of an ancient fortress. Nor have I climbed a path so treacherous, so tormenting, steep, and strewn with stones that roll under the foot of the hiker and all around.

'Tis the only way to Deva Fortress. Once at the castle, you're sweetly rewarded with the view, since you've conquered a mountain resembling a sugar bowl.

Without handholds, without ropes, today the climb is just as hard as it's been for those who built this stronghold, 500 years ago.

The Fortress of Deva (Romanian: Cetatea Devei, Hungarian: Déva vára) is a fortress located in the city of Deva, Hunedoara County, on top of a volcanic hill. It was here that the Dacians had built defence fortifications and an observation point from where they could oversee as far as the forests. The Roman conquerors strengthened the walls and defended this fortification. The trade road that connected Dacia with the rest of the empire, also called the salt road, passed right at the foot of the fortress' hill.

Legendary Deva Fortress.

97

Life and Loss at the Castle

As a child, father and I climbed often to the castle.

That's when I always stood behind the cannons, looked at the crosshairs, and then imagined where the cannonball would hit.

In my mind, I would shake Aunt Margit's kitchen and cause plaster to fall in her soup for the many times she pinched me for not finishing my plate. And make Ferentz's table tremble, causing his inkpot to spill over his homework for tormenting me at school.

When war came I knew where the cannons would hit so I told everyone to take shelter, Aunt Margit and Ferentz included.

98

Monastery Rohia Lapus Came Through a Dream

She laughed running uphill, past the boulders that grow, past Pintea's Oak, bouncing from rock to rock till she reached the one that topped them all. There, she waved and placed her arms above her head, her hands drawing a roof.

How could he build her a monastery tipped on a rock? Reason dictated flat ground.

Yet each night faith, leaving no footsteps behind not even on fresh snow, moved the marking cross atop THAT rock.

The priest prayed by his daughter's grave and teared-up at her memory. Faith had spoken through her memory; a church-on-a-rock it will be then.

Over 150 Transylvanian monasteries were destroyed by General Bukov through the order of Empress Maria Theresa during the 18th century. Afterwards, the first Romanian Orthodox church was built only in 1924 (being the first Orthodox monastery built in Ardeal after 1918) and, until 1990 (the Romanian Revolution) it was the only missionary monastery in the north-western part of the country. This is the story of why it was built.

Rohia Monastery, Târgu Lapuş.

99

Yearning, Mocani Migrating from Transylvania to Dobruja

Theirs was a free life, strolling with their sheep, searching for grass even as far as warm Dobruja. Then returning home, to Transylvania, in time for autumn.

They would descend dressed in their white shirts with high collars and tight pants, *cioareci*, leather boots, and woolly coats. Black hats. Speaking in their slow, emphasized way.

When they couldn't pray at their icons anymore, nor speak their ancestral language, they brought their families along.

To Dobruja.

To live peacefully among Tatars, Lipovanz, Greeks, Turks, Armenians, and Germans.

The *Mocans*, in their white shirts and pants, with black hats, were emigrants. Free.

Long before Dobrogea returned to Romania (in 1878) Transylvanian shepherds, Mocans, travelled here during annual transhumance.

Coming from a land ruled by Hungarians, they discovered this welcoming territory between Danube and the Black Sea where they could speak their ancestral language and worship icons, although it was a land under Turkish ruling. Here they found lush pastures for their sheep and welcoming places to establish new households. Romanian Transylvanian shepherds from Braşov, Făgăraş, Sibiu, and Orăştie settled here alongside Dobrogean Romanians, Turks, Tatars, Gagauzians, Lipovans, Greeks, Armenians and Germans. Here, the Ottoman Empire provided favourable conditions, with taxes that were low or even absent. Some Mocans returned with their sheep to their homelands, while others remained and founded new households. After 1878, when the problem of a serious colonization of Dobrogea was raised, the number of Mocans also increased. Apart from transhumance the Mocans immigrated because of difficult life conditions and lack of human rights they endured in Transylvania, that was then still part of the Austro-Hungarian Empire.

100

In Memory and Heart, Life of a Shepherd

Gramps always took me along, the journey the same, a millennial trek flattened by generations of shepherds. And their dogs.

Fir trees, their stories whispered in the breeze. The wolves, the pastures, the whey cheese. In that order.

The arrival was in early spring, according to the clock of those who look after sheep for a living.

Now that he is gone, his route is an old map that I once knew by heart. Today its memory takes me back to see those landscapes again, where the sheep graze.

Thanks to Gramps I tasted the free life of a shepherd.

101

Bran, a Queen's Desire

The Queen's rooms, as her pain, were hidden from view when one neared Bran Castle. Here, master builders and true carpenters performed their magic transforming the old artillery room into a peaceful expanse.

A prayer room.

And Verona himself promised to bring God's blessings through its murals. In the room where he was to rest for eternity. In his sarcophagus like a cot, young Voivode Mircea, the Queen's youngest son.

While her adopted country and beloved people, the Romanians, endured the great battles of 1916 fighting to fulfil their millennial dream of independence.

The Queen's pain was hidden from view.

From the Queen's balcony, view over Bran's inner court.

102

Zenith of Hope, A Saxon Memory

It was a warm January. The Russians took us from our loved ones, our kinsmen. I hid by the animal fodder, in the forest. I wasn't afraid, alone in the night, because I had a much bigger fear: leaving my children alone.

On the third day my father-in-law said he'll take my place. I couldn't let him. I packed some clothes and food. Hugged my babes.

We left Biertan on foot, like slaves, blessed with good weather and the song of church bells.

For five years they echoed in my mind.

Stray cats and dandelion flowers, that's how I survived.

When Romania signed a peace treaty with the Soviets in 1944, about 100,000 Saxons living in Transylvania (especially Bistriţa) fled. Romania did not expulsed its German-origin population as other countries did. At least 75,000 Biertan Saxons and Swabians (a local German ethnic group) were arrested by the Soviet Army and sent to labour concentration camps in contemporary Ukraine and Siberia, for alleged cooperation with Nazi Germany. For the German ethnic community living in Romania this was the beginning of their end.

103

Riding the Mocanita Train

The train ride assaulted my bones as much as it invaded my nostrils. The wheels, thoroughly checked by the weeltapper, were locked unto the narrow tracks with the stubbornness of an old woman. The wooden bench, crafted from the fir-wood the same train brought from the forest, offered little support.

In the open wagon, as we carved way between evergreen branches and silver streams, too small to leave a mark, I inhaled peppery oil mingled with crisp mountain air.

I was coals and steam. A shadow passing through. Wood among woods. Steel upon steel.

The past, extended into the future.

Mocăniță is a forestry narrow-gauge railway found in Romania in the historical provinces of Maramures, at Vişeu de Sus, Transylvania, Bukovina, and Suceava. The cosy wagons are pulled by a steam-powered locomotive.

Today a mere tourist attraction, the Mocăniţa railway was built over 100 years ago for passengers and cargo services.

104

Quintessential, a Saxon Garden in May

Frau Christa, with her straw hat and matching apron, laboured in her vegetable garden each Saturday morning raking tirelessly, watering, and weeding. In the quiet of the dawn you could only hear her hoe and, sometimes, the snap of the rhubarb.

'Chew fresh one, for rosy cheeks.'

We would sneak into her yard and, through the chicken netting, stir the rooster with a stick. The troublesome singer that knew no holiday.

My favourite hide-and-seek spot was between the rhubarb plants. A secret I kept to myself until today.

Although Fra Christa would share her rhubarb pie with all the children.

Rhubarb has its own food festival in Saschiz village, (*Keisd* in German, *Kisd* in Transylvanian Saxon dialect, *Szászkézd* in Hungarian), located in Mureş County, northeast Transylvania and only 20 km from Sighişoara. Here one can taste, cooked with rhubarb, soup, ice-cream, pie, pizza, cake, jam, and syrup, among other dishes.

Legend goes that the giants who lived here were kind, but disliked loud noises. Whenever humans were noisy, the giants would pick them up to quiet them. Then they would place them back on the ground so humans can spread the word of their near escape. Sometimes the giants would play freebie with flat stones. Later, humans used these stones to pave their streets.

It seems that the rhubarb jam and the milk comfiture were first prepared by these giants too.

Sibiu, traditional costumes and dance.

105

Year-round, Richis Fortified Church

Old George used to appear every morning, half-asleep, by the foot of the tree that rose outside the church yard, where the path curved. He'd lift his old army-hat. Smiled at whoever walked past.

Sometimes, when I went to school at eight in the morning, I would find him lying on the grass, a mass of torn clothes, grey hair, and a beard that shone in the light of dawn, giving out a strong whiff of cheap wine.

Then the winter after the war came sooner.

Under the tree where Old George used to sleep, a mound of snow appeared.

Richiș in Romanian is *Rechesdref* in Transylvanian Saxon dialect, *Reichesdorf* in German, and *Riomfalva* in Hungarian is located in Biertan, Sibiu County. Long ago a monastic order resided here. During Protestant reformation the villagers banished the monks who were forced to leave the community and their church behind. Today this is a Catholic worship place.

Richis fortified church

106

Lindenfeld a Deserted Village in Severin, Banat

Life's echoes of voices, of feet stomping to church on a Sunday morning, of children's laughter, sheep bleating, and dogs barking have long seeped into the ground. They fell between the cracks of broken foundations.

When people left Lindenfeld they took their dreams with them. What's left is a village reclaimed by nature. Tall grass and branches poke through empty window frames. Floorboards watch the sky.

Only the church stands, its roof fixed; its bell still singing, still calling to the souls of those buried in the cemetery.

Ding-dong.

Another spring and new shoots still blossom in this lost village.

Lindenfeld village in Caraş-Severin on Semenic Mountain, Banat County, was colonized with Pemi settlers who arrived from Bohemia and Bavaria during the 18th century. Life blossomed and, soon, prosperous villages such as Wolfswiese (Poiana), Wolfsberg (Gărâna), Weidenthal (Brebu Nou), and Lindenfeld appeared. During the 1980s, when most Germans living in Romania returned to Germany under the harsh Communist regime and its restrictions, this village was deserted.

107

Beyond the Surface, the Statue

He's been waiting a long time. The sun burned to the depths of his brain. Sleet pelted him.

They've put him in the square just for photos.

He was tired of waiting in idleness. His arms ached from stretching out and he now measured the time between sunset and sunrise by the birds resting on them.

From time to time he entertained himself by looking up at the sky, hoping that the next airplane will fly by soon and he could return to where he belonged.

Once he'd been shrapnel. Before that a coin, a nail, a watch's balance wheel.

108

An Emigrant's Dreams, Timişoara

In a factory in Timişoara George weaves the threads of the carpets that will be exported on the west market.

He knows that not a single strand should be out of place, not a shade out of pattern, because this carpet will tell the story of his kin, of their story of survival.

And maybe that, in a German town, his beloved Maria of Ion, who pours coffee for a living, will see the carpet and know that if she does her job well she will have the money she needs to buy the ticket back to her native land.

109

Zero or Infinity, Life Choices

Many years later, when his firing squad days were over, the former colonel thought he found peace amid guilt, shame, and nightmares.

In his pension room, with nothing but his declining health for company, he listened to the sayings of an English cosmologist who explained the theory of multiverses. In his last moments he understood that the existence of another version of himself, one who never entered the army and today taught at a school in a remote village, was possible.

Then he closed his eyes imaging a life he could have chosen.

If he'd only had thought of it.

110

The Székely Potatoe Bread from Covasna

Every evening after kneading the dough *Irinke Neni*, Aunty Irina, makes the sign of the cross above it, says '*Isten segits*', 'God help' in Hungarian, and leaves it to rise until the next day.

Early morning, right after dawn, she would take her apron again and head for the summer-kitchen at the yard's end, by the lilac bush. There, she would arrange the breads in the hot oven where they would bake for almost two hours. The large whitewashed oven swallows ten loaves of bread with its smoky mouth.

The trough stands while breads bake. Or 'they will never rise.'

In Covasna, *Kovászna megye* in Hungarian, lives the second-greatest percentage of Hungarians from Romania, after Harghita. The Hungarians of Covasna are primarily Székelys.

A traditional Szekler potato bread weighs almost two kilograms. It's thick, filling, and it lasts a family of four for two days but if it's warm it will melt before your eyes. It's best enjoyed with a spread with lard, sprinkled with red onions and a pinch of salt and paprika, a delicacy! Know that you can't cut a steaming potato bread with a knife. Tear it in pieces using your hands. It is tradition.

111

The Axis of Brasov, Rope Street

The cobbled stone path glistens like a snake leading the way. The full moon, low in the sky, ventures not past the double-story houses. Tonight, the bright buildings bent inwards, protecting the Rope Street, a slit once made through their midst.

Walls scrape my arms. I walk, yet the buildings seem to glide with me. The slit of light I focus on, the end of the street, remains just as far and narrow.

Shadowed by war and worries, by past quests, the houses to my left and right seem eager for fresh life. Mine.

I suddenly know how it survived.

Carved during the 17th century the main purpose of Rope Street, Braşov, was to ease the firefighters' access when needed. The street measures at its narrowest point 111 centimetres in width and at its widest only 135 centimetres. Today it connects Schei Gate Street and Stag Street.

Rope Street, Brasov, view towards Tampa Mountain.

112

Tihuta Pass or Borgo Pass, the Contemporary Myth of Bistrita

Then.

A mountain path like an emerald belt hugged the curves of Bârgău Mountains whose tree-church sang of life and death.

In summer it became a glistening snake under rain, silver under full moon. Shining so bright underfoot that many dared it. Foolish souls who knew not of the spirits lurking in its woods.

Fall's leaves teared-paved it and, at first snow, the path was locked in winter. Reclaimed by nature, lay hidden under snow till snowdrops smiled again, old bones poked through shining white.

Today.

It's an asphalt route. Many drive it unknowingly and, before they realise, they're out.

Tihuța Pass (in Romanian *Pasul Tihuța* or *Pasul Bârgău*; in Hungarian *Borgói-hágó* or *Burgó*) is a high mountain pass in the Romanian Bârgău Mountains, Eastern Carpathians. It connects Transylvanian Bistrița with Vatra Dornei in Bukovina, Moldava.

If it sounds familiar it might be because 19th century Irish author Bram Stoker mentioned Borgo Pass in his Gothic novel 'Dracula', as the gateway to the realm of Count Dracula.

Tihuța Pass in winter.

113

When Life Had Other Plans

I stopped by the statue one late evening when the traffic was almost non-existent, knowing his grave would be underneath. I sat on the curb, closed my eyes and listened.

First I heard the street noises. Then slowly, very slowly and much later, I heard the forest.

How lonely did he feel here? Away from his civilized world, away from everything that comprised his reality?

No whisper of his mother tongue, or the notes that made up the tunes he grew up with. Even the sky knew different colours here.

He, a poet at heart, while life had other plans.

114

Legend of Cehei Pond, Sălaj

Our stout guide had sunburned cheeks stained with berries. A smile plastered on his face. Was friends with the stray dogs because he'd baptized them. They adored him back.

Fearless too. Till we reached the loch. Only his finger pointed to the church bell rising above the waters.

'ey went to sleep, and never awoke. Waters swallowed 'eir village. You'll get sucked. Don't go 'ere,' he nodded all-knowing.

Red water snakes I thought as he chased to his chores.

I reached the shore of the blackened pond and thought I see, and hear, the church bell ringing for funeral.

Whose?

Uileacu Şimleului in Romanian, *Somlyóújlak* in Hungarian, is a village in Sălaj County northwest Transylvania. Cehei Pond or Uileacul Marsh nearby hides the traces of a mysterious disappearance. It is said that in this place, long ago, there was a village. No one knows how and why the village was covered by waters, yet during sunny days one can still hear the long wailing of the church bell resonating from under the lake, predicting one's fate.

Interior of a country house from Salaj.

115

Old Beliefs on an Old Land, Transylvania

With his snowed hair, jodhpurs, and knee-high boots, this gent doesn't seem the kind who'd believe in witches' cures.

'It's a piece of luck when a stork nests on your rooftop,' his chin shoots to the straws above. 'Bad luck if you knock 'em down.'

We're here to buy our home.

Entering the cottage feels like stepping into a fairy-tale. Stout oak beams, walls lined with rough plaster. A ceramic stove pumping warmth. Shuttered windows peep into the courtyard.

'Don't be alarmed if you hear noises at night-time. That should ward-off vampires,' he gestures to garlic nailed into the plaster.

116

The Hearth, the Heart at Corvin Castle

The fortress' walls still pay the debt left by kings. Their rocks, once enchanted, crumble each day under the rake of weather, the harsh words of time. Wooden doors once loved by craftsmen are turned to dust.

The fickleness of time.

The Queen's chamber is gone, as are her conspiracies. Only the staircase spirals into void.

Yet in this decay a crumb of hope resists. The heart of the castle. The hearth. The kitchen.

With blackened walls that shine like marble, away from the rooms where kings and queens lived in laughter and tears, the kitchen, unknown and unspoiled, survived.

117

A Forest, Alive: Hoia, Cluj

I drove past thicket today. When traffic froze.

Roadside brambles caught my eye. Movement. Something, someone! Rags to the ground. Hair in a tuft.

Then the clouds dropped. Chill swept over. I shivered in the late summer day and smelled ozone, wet wood.

A gush of wind brought the trees alive. Leaves rushed towards me.

The hand clawing at my window had nails as sharp as twigs. Dark as dirt. Stumpy node. Bushy brows. Eyes like deep pools.

'Give it back,' it creaked.

I tasted sour, rotten wood.

'The days forests took over the roads,' the weather bureau will announce.

Over 25% of Romania's territory is covered in forests.

Hoia Forest (Pădurea Hoia in Romanian, Hója-erdö in Hungarian) is found near Cluj-Napoca, northwest Transylvania.

The Oldest Neolithic settlement in Romania was discovered nearby. Could this be an explanation for the lost souls that is said to inhabit this forest?

Hoia Baciu Forest.

List of Illustrations

With thanks to the following photographer for making their work widely accessible (June 2022):
1 Krisztian Matyas, Unsplash / 2 Theodor Vasile, Unsplash / 3 Vanessa Linzenbold, Unsplash / 4-Cuciulat, Wikipedia / 5 Iuliu Illes, Unsplash /6 Iulia Plapsa, Unsplash / 7 Dan-V, Unsplash / 8 Jan Behnisch, Unsplash / 9 PWodicla, Wikipedia / 10 Sergiu Gabriel, Unsplash / 11 Andrada, Wikipedia / 13 Maria Mihaltan, Unsplash / 16 Iuliu Ilies, Unsplash / 17 Daniel Mirlea, Unsplash / 18-Odette Ion, Unsplash / 19 Michael Walk, Unsplash / 20 Patricia Furstenberg / 21 Bogdan Lapadus, Unsplash / 23 Joe Mabel, Wikipedia / 24 Diana Popescu, Wikipedia / 26 Zolti Emeric-Unsplash / 28 S Onisor, Wikipedia / 29 Rachitov, Unsplash / 30 Alina Belascu - Wikipedia / 32 Mircea Solomiea, Unsplash / 34 Ela Vaida, Wikipedia / 37 Cezar Suceveanu, Wikipedia / 39 Daniel Eliashevskyi Unsplash / 40 David Jordan, Unsplash / 43 Ceahlau, Wikipedia / 44 Razvan Popescu, Wikipedia / 44 Adrian Rosco Stef, Unsplash / 45 Andrei Kokelburg, Wikipedia / 46 Bogdan Stanciu, Wikipedia / 47 Horia Varlan,Wikipedia / 48 Marian Mirea,Unsplash / 50 TM Rares, Wikipedia / 51 Andrei Hao, Wikipedia / 52 Nomadic Julien B, Unsplash / 53 Silviu Nastase, Wikipedia / 54 Andrea Dioporco, Wikipedia / 55 Oana Frandes, Wikipedia / 56 Patricia Furstenberg / 57 Otto Schemmel, Wikipedia / 58 Bucium, Wikipedia / 59 MR Tetcu, Wikipedia / 61 Hover Klaudia, Unsplash / 62 Iceberg, Wikipedia / 63 Jonny Gios, Unsplash / 64 Daniel Smith, Unsplash / 66 Patricia Furstenberg / 69 Pag autumn, Wikipedia / 70 Cuiesti, Wikipedia / 72 Roberto Sorin, Unsplash / 74 Otto Scemmel, Wikipedia / 75 Bonita Kondrei, Wikipedia / 77 Mihai Lazar, Unsplash / 79 Rozdel Ion, Wikipedia / 81 Radu Eduard, Wikipedia / 83 Prinslop, Wikimedia / 84 Turda, Wikimda / 86 Patricia Furstenberg / 88 Patricia Furstenberg / 89 Bogdan Ilie, Wikipedia / 93 Emil Pop, Wikipedia / 94 Ela Vaida, Wikipedia / 95 TM Rares, Wikipedia / 96 Deva, Wikipedia / 98 Cosmin Cornea, Wikipedia / 99 George Toma, Unsplash / 101 Nomadic Julien, Unsplash / 103 Elisa Photography, Unsplash / 104 Sibiu, Wikipedia / 105 Richis, Wkipedia / 108 Adrian Rosco Stef, Unsplash / 111 Strada Sforii, Wikipedia / 112 Romanesc Este Latin, Wikipedia / 115 Ramon Salinero, Unsplash / 117 Hoia Baciu, Wikipedia.

ABOUT THE AUTHOR

Patricia Furstenberg is a skilled multi-genre author known for her uplifting, thought-provoking themes and her appealing characters.

With a medical degree behind her, Patricia is passionate about the human mind and the psychology behind it. Her writing echoes the realities of life and is accented by 'creativity and vivid imagery.' She knows how to 'capture the reader's imagination.' Her prolific writing is described as: positive, diverse, crisp, joyful and uplifting.

Ever so proud of her Romanian roots, she initiated the hashtag #Im4Ro, sharing positive stories from Romania.

Patricia lives with her husband, children and dogs in sunny South Africa.

Printed in Great Britain
by Amazon

f9603ec8-57f5-4473-af3c-e678cd800c29R01